The Liberal
Future in
America

Recent titles in
Contributions in Political Science
Series Editor: Bernard K. Johnpoll

The Liberal
Future in
America

ESSAYS IN RENEWAL

EDITED BY
Philip Abbott and Michael B. Levy

Contributions in Political Science, Number 123

GP

GREENWOOD PRESS

Westport, Connecticut
London, England

Library of Congress Cataloging in Publication Data

Main entry under title:

The Liberal future in America.

(Contributions in political science, ISSN 0147-1066 ;
no. 123)
Bibliography: p.
Includes index.
1. Liberalism—United States—Addresses, essays,
lectures. I. Abbott, Philip. II. Levy, Michael B.
III. Series.
JA84.U5L495 1985   320.5′13′0973   84-12834
ISBN 0-313-23761-1 (lib. bdg.)

Library of Congress Catalog Card Number: 84-12834
ISBN: 0-313-23761-1
ISSN: 0147-1066

First published in 1985

Greenwood Press
A division of Congressional Information Service, Inc.
88 Post Road West
Westport, Connecticut 06881

Printed in the United States of America

10 9 8 7 6 5 4 3 2 1

Copyright Acknowledgments

Grateful acknowledgment is made to *The Review of Politics* for
permission to reprint a revised version of Michael B. Levy's "Il-
liberal Liberalism: The New Property as Strategy," *The Review
of Politics* 45, no. 44 (October 1983). Reprinted with permission
from *The Review of Politics*, University of Notre Dame, Notre
Dame, Indiana.

Contents

The Liberal
Future in
America

Philip Abbott and Michael B. Levy

I

Liberalism and Renewal

It has been over a quarter of a century since Louis Hartz confidently claimed that the entire history of the United States could be told only through the symbols and cadences of liberal speech. Whereas the previous generation of American historians had seen our nation's history as a series of conflicts between old elites and rising masses, Hartz was more impressed by the consensus that framed, and thus virtually contained, these conflicts. What might have appeared to the immediate combatants as incompatible differences were really, for Hartz, the full actualization of ideals already present at the American founding. Seen in this way, the New Deal was the twentieth-century oak that had matured from the eighteenth-century American acorn, rather than an alien limb forcibly grafted onto the polity's trunk. Indeed this was a comforting view of American development because it suggested that we possessed a public philosophy—liberalism—that was coherent enough to provide continuity and harmony yet flexible enough to articulate and guide change.

To someone coming of political age since Hartz wrote *The Liberal Tradition in America*, neither the hegemony nor the wisdom of liberalism can be taken for granted. The severe economic dislocations of the past decade, a social agenda still in-

complete despite the promises of the New Deal and Great
Society, and an unsuccessful and unpopular war waged by liberal presidents speaking its rhetoric have done much to undermine liberalism as unquestioned public philosophy.
Moreover, as any reader of the works pouring out of American
universities and journals knows, liberalism has been the favored target of intellectual scorn for an even longer time. Neo-
Marxist and neoconservative writers often have joined hands
to attack the premises of liberal theory and decry the failings
of liberal society. To some extent this is only natural. In a
liberal society, the intellectual's role is that of critic. Predict-
ably, if ironically, the prevailing orthodoxy will be the critics'
most common target. Nevertheless—even after taking normal
intellectual disaffection into account—the most sympathetic
observer must recognize a pervasive feeling that liberalism is
a political stance one increasingly struggles to escape rather
than refurbish.

And the criticism has been quite severe indeed. Marxists
charge that liberalism remains capitalism; it has legitimated
an order of power that can only alienate men and women from
their labor and each other. Exploiting the language of liberty
and equality, these critics assert, liberal society has actually
perpetuated inequality and a one-dimensional servility. When
many cannot find work and countless others despair of finding
work that is compatible with meaning and dignity in their
lives, this analysis cannot be dismissed. On the other hand,
classical conservatives see liberals as having used the rhetoric
of fairness, tolerance, and equality to promote skepticism as
the only permissible epistemological stance. As a consequence,
the ideas of virtue and character appear to be without meaning,
or worse, become subjects of parody. Moreover, both critical
traditions agree that the liberal emphasis on individual life
plans destroys community and shared civic life. Thus, argues
the conservative, the early liberal insistence upon religious
toleration leads inextricably to the contemporary cry to "do
your own thing"; a short skip across conceptual space, no matter
how long in historical time. Through these lenses, the logical
end point of liberalism appears to be solipsism, narcissism, and
the end of vigorous social and political life. Paradoxically, in

its place looms an increasingly penetrative state as the sole guarantor of order.

The contemporary dismissal of liberalism has two different starting points. Some writers consciously have removed themselves from any connection with the tradition that they criticize. Others, even if unconsciously, mimic the liberal views they attack. Those belonging to the former group, whether to the left or to the right of liberalism, have felt free to reduce the successes of liberal societies to an accident of abundant conditions now necessarily past, or conversely to a residual, pre-liberal moral capital which, they charge, liberal culture has squandered as its control has become more complete. On the other hand, when considering those who direct their criticism at contemporary liberal *practice*, Hartz still offers us an important reminder. Much of what passes as criticism of liberalism is really liberalism in another guise, critiques which draw on some liberal values to dismiss or downplay others. This is all too possible given the precarious balance between liberty and equality, ambition and civic friendship, rights and obligations that any liberal theory and polity must strive to achieve.

This proclivity suggests alternative hypotheses about the liberal future: (1) that it is a tradition too filled with conflicting premises and values to offer coherence to the contemporary world, or (2) that it is a tradition of sufficient complexity and reflexive capacity, however frustrating, which remains capable of explaining a changing world and guiding action within it. Which alternative is correct is not at all clear—perhaps least of all to those who still call themselves liberals.

Often more impressed by the limits of the existing order than its possibilities, the contemporary liberal's outlook is far different from that of the tradition's early twentieth-century American representatives—Progressives as well as those whom R. Allan Lawson has called "independent liberals." Writers like John Dewey were confident that free inquiry and liberated intelligence offered them a future that was theirs to be made. The liberal community they envisioned was to resemble the web of relationships that characterized the scientific community. Scientists were independent minds, yet they owed their ability to explore the frontiers of knowledge to institutions that had nurtured them. They, in turn, freely cooperated with others in the common search for truth.

To our contemporary ear, the metaphor of citizens as scientists searching for common truths rings with a quaint naivete. The world we have come to understand is more David Truman's than John Dewey's, more the interest group free-for-all described in *The Governmental Process* than the nurturing association advocated in *Liberalism and Social Action*. Too often political actors search for coalitions of advantage rather than common truths, and merely pillage the rhetoric of *Communitas* to support their ambition. Even if one accepts the bargaining process as necessary to the open society, he would need grossly misplaced faith in a pluralist "invisible hand" to connect such individual and group ambition to the common good.

Reticence is now the norm, especially so when liberals confront the American welfare state, their central institutional heritage and the most common focus for critics of all persuasions. From differing perspectives, opponents of the welfare state maintain that it destroys individual self-reliance, acts as an agent of social control that systematically destroys true democratic initiative, and masks privilege in the name of needs. These sentiments are often coupled with a rejection of bureaucracy and complex organization which may be articulated by civic theorists on the Left but ironically echoes the nostalgic individualism of those on the American Right. Liberals do not so much disagree as simply recoil from any available alternative. With a realization that the comparison is a limited one, contemporary American liberals have assumed the role of the "rational republicans" of Weimar Germany. A liberal regime is supported as a kind of second or third best choice justified only in the absence of other historical choices. Such passive acquiescence is hardly the basis for a liberal renascence and can do little to revitalize a public philosophy.

Yet, however nettlesome, the problems of the welfare state do not pose the most severe *philosophical* dilemma for liberalism. Were confidence in the liberal understanding of human life more robust, we would be more willing to discuss the problems of modern individualism, democratic politics, and economic growth within the contours of the liberal tradition. This is not to suggest that a flagging economy burdened by liberal commitments yet still unable to fulfill its aspirations should not have called the truth of liberal analysis into question. Indeed it is inevitable and even required by the very respect for science and pragmatic analysis that is part of the liberal tradition. But it is to argue that problems of execution and unintended consequences do not require abandoning fundamental values and beliefs *unless* the latter have themselves been shown to be faulty and the cause of problems we face.

From the perspective of liberalism's long-term health, it is this attack on foundations far more than the attacks on the performance of institutions which provides the greatest challenge. To accept such recriminations is to will that the next generation be unable to consider this tradition's virtues. It is to assert the bankruptcy of liberalism rather than the partial and usable truths of other traditions. It is to break the intellectual bonds that connect American generations.

Yet under a barrage of criticism, one cannot be faulted for wondering what, if anything, is left in liberal ideas that is worthy of consideration. The answer, however tentative, begins with liberalism's original appeal. And it is here that we must return.

The overwhelming fact of modern life remains our diversity, and it is in this perception that liberalism takes its beginning. The very existence of self-reflective social sciences reminds us that in the modern world identity as well as behavior is problematic. From its origins in the political writings of bourgeois and Protestant dissenters, through the strivings of twentieth-century trade unionists and minority groups, liberal theory has attempted to accommodate this fact. As early as John Locke, liberal writers conceived of the essence of the individual human condition as standing independent of organized political life and social convention. As an expression of their natural condition, individuals asserted their equal right to interpret the laws of nature and their relation to it. A century later, Immanuel Kant could insist on the absolute duty to respect free personality—so much so "that no one could compel me to be happy in accordance with his conception of the welfare of others." Thus liberal philosophers have painted the individual as a separate and undetermined subject; as a consequence they have charged the modern individual with the task of fashioning a life in a world stripped of organic unity and inherited meaning.

Yet this does not exhaust the liberal project. Despite so radical and even antiseptic a portrayal of every person's distinct individuality, liberals have also persisted in developing a conceptual basis for legitimate authority and shared public life. Liberals have promoted equal rights to protect the individual, but also majoritarian democracy to give voice to the "public" will. As an expression of individual liberty, they have advocated private property and the market, but in turn tempered its worst effects with the welfare state. Kantian respect for individual personality has meant respecting the right to autonomy but it has also meant guaranteeing the means to develop a free personality. To ensure that freedom is more than a set of mere formal privileges, liberals have argued for greater equality; but they have also defended the inequality of wealth and power to which an open society has given rise. Again the inevitability of contradiction or at least disabling tension is apparent. At its best, the liberal vision has taken the diverse facts of modernity and created an order which is capable of supporting each individual's purposive journey through life. At its worst, liberal theory simply mirrors the diversity of liberal societies and resembles a Babel of competing claims to life, liberty, and happiness.

Despite this potential for internal disorder, any defender of liberalism must cherish its history of repeated support for the rights of individuals to a life of personal freedom and growth. The history of the twentieth century bears witness to the many altars upon which men and women have been sacrificed in the names of national glory, economic transformation, or fraternity. The refusal of most liberals to condone such activities and the lack of support that liberal symbols can provide to repressive movements speaks to the tradition's continued importance. While one need not accept that the experience or even the idea of liberal freedom fulfills all that one might mean by that term, the capacity of liberal theory and politics to defend individual diversity, and to do so in ways that are not frozen in time, remains impressive. This is especially true when viewed against alternative formulations.

The liberal tradition's willingness to accept diversity and thus its uneasiness with coercive political reconstruction has clearly observable roots in such theoretical writings as Locke's *Letters on Toleration*, John Milton's *Areopagitica*, and Roger Williams' *Bloody Tenent*. Unfortunately, this individualistic emphasis has led liberals away from a consideration of the many social experiences which have been supportive of individual autonomy. Thus a source of strength also forms a basic weakness in liberal philosophy. In a sense such a weakness is curious, in that the genesis of liberal individualism can be found in the struggles of men and women who had definite group identities as members of churches, guilds, professions, and classes. Yet liberals have been unable to integrate this historical experience into their theoretical conceptions of individualism despite the attempts by theorists such as T. H. Green and John Dewey. A return to their project is essential if liberals are to revive the idea of individualism and complement and complete it with a richer understanding of the social nature of human personality.

The critique of liberalism as an atomistic philosophy usually has been directed toward classical liberals who left little room for public or political action. These same theorists also seemed to ignore the severe effects of economic inequality on the development of individual potential and political equality, so that the case against liberal atomism usually converged with the case against the classical liberal acceptance of inequality.

However, in their tendency to reduce humans to atoms, and in their related inability to appreciate the social and communal aspects of human development, some egalitarian liberals share more in common with classical liberals than at first seems apparent. The egalitarian who pursues busing as the only solution to the problem of school and neighborhood integration without any sensitivity to the history of meaning of neighborhood schools, the feminist whose revolt against patriarchy ripens into a wholesale attack on the family, and the civil libertarian who refuses any role for community groups in textbook selection are surely not the liberal atomists of Spencerian

liberalism. But they are atomists nonetheless. They reduce
each of us to singular categories of identity, based on whatever
is the relevant criterion of the moment, and then feel free to
rearrange lives accordingly. As much as the militant defender
of the absolute right of property, radical egalitarians often ignore the importance of cultural and social life in each individual's definition of self. In this way the state as agent of
egalitarian reforms—as readily as the absentee-owned corporation—becomes an external force imposing unchosen outcomes upon the lives of individuals. Taken to an extreme, this
contributes to the demise of conditions which have nurtured
the free personality.

To be sure, traditional social forms or institutions may conflict
with equal opportunity, equal rights, or even simple decency
in ways that liberals must oppose. Nevertheless, liberals must
see beyond their penchant for conceiving of individuals as simply full-blown rational creatures emerging from the state of
nature and be more sensitive to the actual experiences through
which we have become ourselves. Men and women come to their
identities in families, churches and synagogues, unions, schools,
and neighborhoods, as well as in consciousness-raising sessions
and reform caucuses. The need for heightened sensitivity to
what neoconservatives call mediating institutions is important
for liberals not because conservatives have taken over a cluster
of issues, but rather because liberals need to understand their
own experience. Such institutions, whether they are chosen
like the reform caucus or inherited as with one's church, are
the very expressions of our diversity and subjectivity, and need
to be reintegrated into the liberal's ideas of how to achieve
liberty, equality, and justice. They are schools for learning the
mixture of social cooperation and individualism that a liberal
political philosophy must hope to nurture.

The reintegration of a conception of group life to liberal theory may also help liberals to refocus their commitment to the
welfare state. Liberals need to again ask about the effects of
their agenda on the abilities of men and women to raise families, or on the abilities of neighborhoods to handle local problems. Approaching the welfare state in this fashion allows
liberals to conceive of and design a welfare state that is neither

atomistic nor monolithically collectivist. It also helps the liberal shape programs that foster a fuller individualism nurtured through mediating institutions rather than in opposition to them. It is a false liberalism indeed that sees itself in a constant war with all vestiges of traditional culture or local actions.

Having said all this, one must readily admit that the boundaries between desirable and undesirable actions are not easy to draw, nor should they be. It is quite possible that a given neighborhood school provides an important focus for a community's life and at the same time maintains *de facto* segregation with a shocking gusto. One need not suggest that the liberal ignore the very dark side of community life, but rather that he or she frame a response with the goal of a more egalitarian and liberal *community* in mind. The goal must be to expand as far as possible the positive experiences of social life and thus create greater opportunity for individual development and growth, rather than to destroy it for all equally. Utilizing this approach, we are less likely to view individualism as a goal necessarily in conflict with equality or to view both individualism and equality as always in conflict with community. Perhaps then a sense of balance and proportion can be added to a liberal rhetoric to which so many seem unable to relate.

This, finally, is what these essays are about: the difficulty of defining a liberal perspective in a complex world for which liberalism has neither lost its relevance nor proven its adequacy. While not agreeing to a single point of view, the contributors to this volume each speak to this need. Many find in past liberal tendencies a simplification of experience that is mechanistic or reductivist to an extent that harms the liberal project. While some contributors decry old liberal practices and beliefs and others attempt to define new liberal directions, each nevertheless exhibits tendencies which one might call liberal whether or not choosing to accept that label.

The first essay argues strenuously for the need to reconceive the "liberty" that is at the core of liberal thinking. Glenn Tinder contends that "society is always in some degree morally degraded" and thus selfhood can never be realized by obedience to public norms. Exercising liberty will not be in harmony with all other actions, nor the actions of all others. Alienation in some instances becomes the proper condition of man, and we must strive to integrate this tragic fact into a mature liberal theory. Thus Tinder consciously rejects the utopian, and perhaps enlightenment, side of liberalism. At the same time he offers a defense of a mature liberalism that is rooted in a deep set of convictions about the irreducible condition of human beings.

Philip Abbott's essay "Liberalism and Social Invention" seems to return to a familiar theme: reform. Although Abbott's "social invention" may not be as much the product of conscious design as reform or social engineering, it is a concept that points to the constant possibility of rational change. Yet, in its modest scope and in its essential willingness to emerge out of experience and shared history, a "social invention" falls purposefully short of attempting to mold "new men." Abbott calls for "social inventions" appropriate to a liberal society that can mediate between the powerful and penetrative institutions of the state and the economy and argues that, "a world rich in sociability" is not one that is devoid of individuality. While more utopian in spirit than Tinder, Abbott similarly sounds the liberal theme of the impossibility of fully joining individual actions to the whole. Accordingly, in making the case for a rich and diverse social realm, Abbott suggests a liberal response to alienation that is careful to avoid totalist and utopian illusions.

The project of reinvigorating traditional social structures is emphasized by Jean Bethke Ehlstain. Marxist and liberal feminists alike, she argues, have been "captured" by "ultra-liberalism," that is, a severe atomism that defines the self in opposition to others. This uncritical acceptance of classical liberal premises *in extremis* cripples feminism and, even in its socialist and Marxist variants, ties it to an individualism that is foreign to traditional female experiences. Ehlstain calls for a reinvigorated liberalism "acquainted with human tragedy, sometimes awed by human triumph." Only by freeing ourselves from "thin" conceptions of individualism can liberals and feminists alike hope to pursue freedom and civic virtue alike.

Robert Booth Fowler applies a similar analysis to liberal attitudes toward religion and religious community. Fowler rejects two traditional liberal views of religion, one stemming from an enlightenment distrust of the supernatural, the other from a sociological tradition emphasizing civil religion. Fowler does not deny that religion may have legitimated democratic institutions, as the civil religionists argue, but this misses its most significant contribution. Similarly, religious communities may be united around a shared conception of the transcendent but their contribution to the secular and mundane are most significant. By providing "an alternative to the liberal order" religion offers a refuge from liberal skepticism and individualism. In the long run this provides functional support for a liberal society and at the same time compensates for that society's incompleteness. Liberals must make an effort to understand the religious experience, suggests Fowler, and integrate it into their practical philosophy.

Alan Stone's essay "Justifying Regulation" shifts the focus of the anthology away from social life and into the economic realm. Nevertheless, he begins with an analysis of economic individualism and points to the necessity of completing it with a public dimension. Stone treats the neoclassical and property rights schools sympathetically, yet demonstrates the inability of the market to achieve fully either efficiency or equity. By offering coherence to disparate defenses of regulation, Stone offers a counter for what he calls a "tidal wave" of antiregulatory sentiment. His sympathetic treatment of neoclassical political economy reminds us of the virtues of liberal individualism, while his concise discussion of its limits reinforces the book's larger argument about the public and social elements of a mature liberal theory.

Michael B. Levy's "Liberty, Property, and Equality" also takes a look at contemporary liberal attitudes toward political economy by focusing on certain egalitarian directions that have been popular since the mid-1960's. Levy is critical of the constitutional law doctrine of the "new property" which has used classical liberal rhetoric about property rights to legitimate public assistance or "welfare." Although Levy is sympathetic to the liberal project of balancing liberty and equality to as great a degree as possible, he warns that the attempt to redefine public grants as property breaks down any *conceptual* grounds for a state/society distinction. While satisfying egalitarian goals, it savages liberal ones and leaves the liberal egalitarian without the positive liberty that he hopes to extend to all. Liberal egalitarians must remember that they are liberals as well as egalitarians and conceive of the welfare state accordingly.

Questions of foreign policy inevitably present problems for liberal theory. A theory that takes the individual as its basic unit of analysis necessarily has difficulty in handling so unitary and collective a notion as the sovereign state. Self-determination applied to individuals may conflict directly with self-determination applied to a nation. For example, national self-determination seems to demand the renunciation of intervention by foreign powers, yet the commitment to individual human rights may require it. James C. Dick's "American Liberalism and the Use of Force" tackles some of these difficult problems. Dick connects the argument that liberalism must consider individuals as social beings defining themselves in social structures to the requirement that liberals accept the "legitimacy of the state and state system." Only then can we chart a reasonable course between millenial demands for unilateral disarmament and apocalyptic fantasies of nuclear war fighting. In many respects, his analysis—if not the conclusion—is the most striking and controversial one in the book.

The anthology ends on a very political note. How can a liberal electoral coalition be rebuilt? David B. Hill's answer is far from sanguine. The number of people who define themselves as liberal has declined, Hill notes, and many who call themselves "liberal" have negative feelings about traditional liberal policies and traditional liberal coalition partners. Nonetheless, Hill finds an as yet unarticulated "public interest liberalism" emerging from survey research data. He holds out the possibility that expressed public concern for education and public health offers liberal candidates an opening around which to organize a liberal agenda. This requires a subtle shift from interest groups' liberalism to a more public liberalism designed to meet commonly held individual needs. But to what extent this is practicable, and compatible with the identities and needs of groups, is difficult to say.

It may be, as Isaiah Berlin once mused, that liberalism is only the late fruit of capitalist civilization, an ideal which "posterity will regard with curiosity, even sympathy, but with little comprehension." Each of the writers in this collection implicitly raises this issue. But at the same time each also appeals to a liberal vision that is historically untried. Perhaps it is on these terms that the basis for a liberal renewal can be built.

Glenn Tinder

II

Liberalism and Liberty

My argument is simply that the principle of liberty rests on a tragic view of human existence, that this is not understood by American liberals, and that the result is an inability to deal with political reality. Liberty is inadequately defined and defended. The twentieth-century crisis of liberty thus consists not only in the number and strength of its opponents but also in the philosophical misjudgments of its friends.

The truth underlying the ideal of liberty is that society is always in some degree morally degraded. Whether society means government, private institutions, or merely neighbors, it is something against which an individual needs protection. In even the best society a human being is more or less an alien. If that were not so, if one were fully at home in society, then liberty would not be needed. Selfhood could be achieved through obedience, conformity, and participation. To be uncompromisingly oneself would be the same as being unreservedly a member of society. A sphere set apart for thoughts and actions pleasing to no one but their author would not be necessary. Liberty is "insupportable," as Dostoevsky asserts,[1] because it is inseparable from alienation. The view of human existence underlying the principle of liberty is tragic in that it postulates an incurable breach between a human being and the organized humanity surrounding him.

This view of liberty is not necessarily an expression of individualism. It may be that the only legitimate purpose of liberty lies in uncoerced relationships and that the goal of life is community. But society is not community (I shall try to show in a moment why this is so) and one whose life is simply a pattern provided by society cannot be himself even if the self, by nature or destiny, is at one with all other selves.

In failing to see clearly and take seriously the tragic incongruity of society and self, liberals necessarily fail to understand the conditions of liberty. Liberals, of course, are not all of one type. The deepest difference among them concerns the economic role of government. This is the difference dividing original liberalism, formed according to the principles of classical economics, and the reformist liberalism of such presidents as Franklin Roosevelt and Harry Truman. As everyone knows, these are very different schools of thought. But both support the principle of liberty and I shall try to show that both fail, in similar fashion, to understand the conditions of liberty. This is a factor, if I am not mistaken, in rendering so often unsatisfactory the alternatives America's two liberal parties place before the voters.

Two major assumptions underlie my argument and these must be stated at the outset. The first concerns the status of liberty in relation to other values and has been forcefully set forth in the writings of Isaiah Berlin.[2]

The values we pursue are diverse and inharmonious. This implies that liberty is not the sole value we should cherish. Nor is it the source of all true values, so that in gaining liberty we would gain all else. On the contrary, there are other values both logically distinct and practically separable from liberty. Often these other values are more or less in conflict with one another and with liberty. Examples come readily to mind: industrial productivity, national security, justice, democracy, and safe streets in the inner cities. Scarcely a moment's reflection is needed to see that attaining one of these values might entail the partial sacrifice of others and of liberty in particular. Thus national security during both world wars required a mobilization of population and resources which entailed considerable limits on personal liberty; justice, as Plato argued and as consideration of a problem such as the status of minority races in America shows, may require governmental acts that are neither willed by the people nor wholly congruent with individual liberty; democracy, as illustrated by the execution of Socrates, may drastically curtail personal freedom; and crime rates could probably be reduced were we willing to neglect due process. A recent best-selling book was entitled *Having It All*.[3] It may be doubted whether having it all is possible for any individual, even in the most fortunate circumstances; it is certainly not possible for any society.

It should be noted that this assumption does not presuppose relativism. If it did, it would be a rather trivial assumption. The values which clash when policy is made are authentic values—ends which society ought to pursue. Good comes into conflict with good, and the sacrifices which have to be made are moral.

The second assumption underlying my argument is that society is a system organized for action and that action cannot be morally pure. Society exists in order to accomplish certain purposes, above all the protection and exploitation of a part of the earth. Society is first of all a military and economic organization. When these material functions are in some measure fulfilled, then spiritual purposes can be pursued. But always society exists to accomplish particular ends and the members of society have to be induced or forced to support these ends. In a civilized society much depends on persuasion and habit and relatively little on force. But in all cases power of some kind must be used, and individuals must be treated as means to social ends. People today are so desirous of social action, as in programs of reform, that the moral deprecation of persons that is inherent in action—and in society as a system of action—is persistently neglected. Yet it is undeniable. One way to see this is simply to observe that no action can be taken without using power, even when such power is purely persuasive rather than coercive, and even when it is used for the most impeccable purposes. Action is inescapably a way of making people serve predetermined ends. It is a way of using them, however good the purposes may be for which they are used.

These two assumptions, it will be apparent, imply that society is unavoidably more or less base. It is in essence a set of relatively degraded relationships. It may allow for, but it cannot consist in, the spontaneity and love which always come immediately to mind when we try to conceive of ideal relationships. This is inherent in the very ends it pursues. A rational society never pursues the good as such, because the good is made up of diverse and conflicting values. The worst societies are those that ignore the conflict of values and pursue what is conceived to be a comprehensive and absolute good. For such societies, liberty can be seen only as allowing people to stand aside from or even resist the attainment of the final and inclusive human good. It is bound to be seen as indefensible.

Even if values were not in conflict, however, society would be more or less base since it is a system of action, viewing people as means to serve its ends. The state, whereby power is deliberately organized and used, is not the polar opposite of society, as is sometimes thought. Rather it reveals the essence of society. The things that are done on lower levels subtly and even sometimes unconsciously are done by the state in full clarity of consciousness and if necessary by force.

Much utopian and radical thought consists primarily in trying to show that the moral inadequacy of society does not belong to its essence. For example, according to a theme voiced as early at least as the Periclean Age in Greece, not all societies, but only large societies, are necessarily base. Society can be fully human by being small. Collective life can become cooperative rather than coercive, it is held, by reducing its scale. Many socialists and democrats in modern times have renewed this theme.

In Marxism, humanity and society are reconciled in a different way. It is held that not society in its essence but society divided between exploiting anad exploited classes is the source of the degradation of persons. The division of classes is in turn conditioned by an insufficiency of wealth which forces people to compete for the means of livelihood. Hence the progress of technology, by increasing wealth (and ultimately by giving rise to the cooperative patterns of production required for the effective use of a highly developed technological order), liberates men from conflict. It liberates them from the conflict of values because it enables them to rise above the selfishness—basically a class selfishness—which is inherent in poverty; in doing this it makes it possible for power-relationships to wither away. Society becomes identical with community.

The former approach is primarily political, the latter primarily economic. On one side it is held that the inhumanity of society can be eliminated through decentralization, on the other through economic development. Most liberals and reformers today probably embrace a combination of these two approaches.

The issues presented are far too large to be argued here. It can, however, be noted here that even casual inspection enables one to see how dubious both approaches are. As for the political approach, while small societies have advantages, such as possibilities of personal contact among citizens, firsthand familiarity with common problems, and participatory democracy, the converse also is true. Large societies have advantages over small ones: economic diversification, cultural breadth and variety, powers of self-defense. The close and oppressive atmosphere of village and small-town life is a commonplace of social commentary. It does exist, however, and it should inhibit reformers from so casually assuming as they often do that smallness is the key to overcoming the alienation of the individual in society.

As for the economic approach, our experience with technology is as yet very brief and we cannot be sure what it will do to human life. It no doubt contains both dangers and opportunities which we are unaware of. But the Marxist assumption that it will finally open the doors to liberty and community is not wholly credible, for this is not what it has done so far and it is not apparent how it can be done. The organization of technology requires scientific expertise, specialization, and managerial control. It requires hierarchy and discipline. At least it has required them so far, and there is nothing to suggest that these necessities—which admittedly can be modified and restrained—can ever be eliminated. Also, technology increases in countless ways the powers of surveillance and control in the hands of dominant groups. In short, the plausible view is that technology renders society far more threatening than it has been in earlier ages.

How is it that so manifest and stubborn a fact as the alien character of society has been so widely neglected and denied? There are probably a number of reasons, such as our reluctance to acknowledge the tragic character of the human situation and our distraction by the conveniences and comforts of industrial abundance. But I think it is legitimate to see one reason in particular as being decisive in our age. That is ideology.

I understand an ideology to be a doctrine framed and propagated in order to mobilize large numbers of people for action. Probably any social philosophy can be turned into an ideology. Conservatism can, even though the mass action it seeks is simply support for the existing order. An ideology cannot be altogether true, as I will try to show, because it necessarily distorts and simplifies. But an ideology might be based on a true philosophy. What makes it an ideology is not its content but its purpose and use and the impact these have on its form.

The purpose of an ideology is twofold, according to my definition. It is first that of mobilizing large numbers of people. This cannot readily be accomplished without falsifying the future. Since values are in conflict, every possible course of action contains drawbacks. No social philosophy can show the way to all good things. But what a true social philosophy cannot do, an ideology must ordinarily pretend to do. It claims that the program for which it calls will solve all major problems. At least tacitly, it denies the conflict of values. This is easily verified. Neither on the right nor on the left do ideological spokesmen admit that actions they prescribe will leave society still facing serious dilemmas. On the contrary, they project the realization of a good that is definitive because it comprehends all major values. How often has one heard a socialist deplore the conformity that is apt to accompany equality or a conservative lament the injustices inseparable from ancient, cherished traditions? To put it simply, the masses cannot readily be mobilized by presenting a tragic vision of life. Ideologies therefore suppress the tragic elements in our consciousness.

The second purpose of an ideology is action. It is a doctrine designed to induce people to act or at the very least to acquiesce in the actions of their leaders. This purpose, too, leads to falsification. Action is depicted as morally pure—not only noble in intent and beneficent in results but also free of moral ambiguities in itself. Its involvement with power and hence with objectification of persons is ignored or obscured. The reason for this is apparent: people can ordinarily be induced to act only if action is made to seem righteous and exhilarating. The tragic inseparability of action and guilt is a condition at odds with the intrinsic intent of an ideology.

An ideology may advocate preserving society or changing it; in the latter case, it may advocate changes of various kinds. But it always calls for measures to secure a certain kind of society and it does this in order to arouse multitudes of human beings. It is thus driven to moral simplification: an actual or prospective society is envisioned as unambiguously good and the measures designed to secure it as wholly right and beneficial. The tragic sense of existence is extinguished.

Our own time has seen an upsurge of ideological passion. This is partly because great multitudes are more powerfully present on the political scene than ever before in history; it is partly because modern men are more confident than ever before of their capacity to act effectively on a vast historical scale. And it is probably related to the decline in the prevalence and intensity of Christian faith. There is a longing for paradise which Christianity sublimated through the idea of an eschatological kingdom—a paradise which would unfailingly be realized, but only with the end of history. The loss of that transcendental expectation has naturally caused the paradisiacal longing to become historical and earthly. The ideologies, of course, do not all speak explicitly of paradise. But they do, conservative and radical alike, respond to the desire to believe that a state of human life unmarred by serious evils can be achieved here and, if not now, soon. There is no doubt an ideological tendency in human nature—a tendency to render our beliefs into forms that are simple and apparently practical and that offer prospects of earthly power and enjoyment. But the ideological temptation, as one might call it, seems particularly strong in our time.

Americans in some ways do not seem like a people very much

disposed toward ideology. They lack the conscious class antag-
onisms which in Europe have contributed to ideological thinking; they also, in their practical-mindedness, are largely free
of the kind of abstract intellectualism which sharpens and
dramatizes ideological differences. In other ways, however,
Americans are spontaneously ideological. They are worldly,
historically optimistic, and given to action. These qualities necessarily characterize anyone committed to an ideology. America may sometimes have seemed to be beyond ideology because
there have been no competing ideologies. As so often noted,
practically all Americans are liberals of one kind or another.
But competition is not essential to ideological thinking. The
truth is that Americans have been no more immune than other
peoples to the ideological temptation, with the result being that
the idea of liberty itself has been subjected to an ideological
transformation.

By this I mean simply that liberty has come to be conceived
as one among a harmonious set of ideals defining a society that
is definitively good and realizable through action. Liberty is
thus removed from the context of a tragic view of existence. In
this way, ostensibly held in high esteem and sought by everyone, liberty is basically misunderstood. Let us first examine
the way in which the ideological transformation of liberty has
come about.

Originally liberalism, as embodied in the doctrine of laissez-
faire, harmonizes liberty and other values by conceiving of
liberty as the source of all major values. Liberty is primarily
economic. It is understood as an absence of restrictions on producing, selling, buying, and hiring. In typical versions of laissez-faire liberalism it is held that economic liberty, at least in
the right circumstances, will bring about maximum productivity, a fair distribution of wealth, and industrial progress. It
will also allow liberty in other areas, as in thought and culture,
to flourish. Economic liberty gives us access to the comprehensive set of values constituting a good society.

I am of course not speaking here of limited reliance on market
mechanisms. The tendency in that direction now is almost universal. It is not in itself ideological but is often a tactic employed
by people committed to ideologies other than original liberalism.

Those committed to the liberal ideology as structured by the concept of a market economy typically bring out certain aspects of existence—acquisitiveness, competition, and the terrible penalties of sloth and failure. Indeed, they are the authors of what was once referred to as "the dismal science." Their science, however, is not tragic. Its dismal features supposedly accord with both nature and justice. And the overall result of its practice is held to be a society in which all of the values men can legitimately desire—wealth, justice, and liberty—will be achieved. And not only are the diversity and conflict of values obscured and denied. So are the moral ambiguities of action. Man is conceived of as an economic being whose nature is realized in the realms of industry and finance. The fact that not all can thus realize themselves is thought to accord with natural justice. I am, of course, not claiming that every classical economist was unaware of these moral shadows; John Stuart Mill, to name but one, is evidence that this was not so. What I am claiming rather is that an awareness of moral shadows— a tragic sense of things—did not enter into the essence of the doctrine.

Someone might argue, however, that with liberals of a different kind, reformist liberals, a consciousness of moral ambiguities did enter into the essence of liberal doctrine. Such liberals denied that all significant values flow from liberty for economic enterprise. They showed that liberty itself, as a general amplitude of life, was destroyed by laissez-faire. Their insight can be described in part in terms of a more complicated view of liberty: it might be enhanced by governmental restrictions on the main centers of economic power. But their insight also was that liberty is meaningless apart from a context in which values other than liberty are enjoyed—values such as economic security, political democracy, and a measure of equality. Does not reformist liberalism, then, transcend ideological simplifications?

It does not, in my opinion, although it introduces a pattern of simplification very different from that of original liberalism. Reformist liberalism does not assume that liberty is *at the source* of all other major values. It assumes rather that liberty is *in harmony* with all other values. It assumes, for example, that economic security can be achieved in a way that will enhance rather than interfere with liberty. It ignores the possibility that economic security for all, even though perhaps well worth the price, might require restrictions on liberty (for example, to check adequately on welfare fraud or to assure tenure in jobs) which no liberal could regard as insignificant. Likewise, reformist liberals assume that the growth of economic democracy and equality can only redound to the benefit of liberty. That it might rather tend to cement everyone into patterns of conformity and comfort, either nullifying or trivializing liberty, and thus fulfilling the forbodings of earlier liberals such as Alexis de Tocqueville, is another possibility liberals have never in our time taken seriouisly. That the broad goals of reformist liberalism are both morally valid and practically feasible can now be taken as unquestionable. Even leaders of the Republican party in the United States do not seriously question them in principle. What does need attention is the relationship of these goals to other morally valid goals, particularly to liberty. It may be said that with the resurgence of original liberalism under Ronald Reagan this has happened. The trouble is, however, that it has happened under the aegis, not of a tragic view of existence, but of another liberal ideology.

Reformist liberals are as untroubled by the moral ambiguities of action as are original liberals. This can be seen in the atmosphere of pragmatic exuberance that prevailed in the White House during Franklin Roosevelt's first term or during John F. Kennedy's short presidency. There was, to be sure, an experimentalism that reflected a consciousness of the possible failure of particular measures. But that even the best measures place their authors in inherently dubious power relationships and entail undesirable consequences is a tragic premise of a kind that men at the summits of national life in 1933 and 1961 were temperamentally incapable of entertaining.

The only major issue between reformist and original liberals, it may be said, has been: who should act? Each has had its favored group of agents, on the one side government and unions, on the other side corporate executives and financiers.

Many kinds of blindness—incurred, for the most part, by both schools of liberalism—were created when the ideal of liberty was transformed into liberalism. There was political blindness, for example. This consisted in an insensitivity to the serious and unavoidable defects in all programs and measures and in an unconsciousness of the grave imperfections that must characterize even the best societies. There was moral blindness, the failure to realize that the most common and difficult choices are not between good and evil but between good and good, and that those who make choices for whole societies cannot avoid guilt.

There was a metaphysical blindness which may at first not be so obvious. Ideologies are always in spirit, and usually in principle, worldly. They are concerned with what can be done here and now, and in order to move the masses to action they emphasize the possible harmony of worldly life and ease of worldly action. Hope is construed in terms of earthly satisfaction and success. I do not mean to hint that liberals should be committed to some doctrinal religion. The issue is not doctrinal commitment but a sense of our ignorance of the ultimate sources and ends of human life and of the consequent mystery that encompasses and pervades our existence. Liberals have typically been insensitive in this respect. They have had little awareness of transcendence. This is an aspect of their lack of tragic consciousness. It is probably impossible to assign any specific religious meaning to a tragic drama by Sophocles or Shakespeare; but no one witnessing or reading such a drama can miss the impression of transcendence which it communicates. Liberals have seemed to draw no impression of this kind from their lives in history. One may see this simply by comparing the mood and demeanor even of so great a liberal as Franklin Roosevelt—a man acquainted with profound distress both in his personal life and in the nation he governed—with Abraham Lincoln.

My argument, simply stated, is that this manifold blindness—political, moral, and metaphysical—amounted to an inability to perceive the realities amid which liberty had to be defined and sustained. The ideal of liberty, as we have seen, calls for the protection of the individual against society. It assumes that society is in some measure alien and threatening. This is the sense in which liberty is founded on a tragic view of human existence. But ideologies, in order to prepare large numbers of people for action, present prospects of a good society, thus denying that society is necessarily alien and threatening. Ideologies are never tragic. Thus when the ideal of liberty was transformed into liberalism, it was displaced from its proper philosophical and spiritual context. The consequence, for supporters of liberty, was that their grasp of reality was seriously weakened. This means that their very capacity for governance was jeopardized. The final step in my argument is to examine this consequence—a consequence which I believe is reflected in the moral and spiritual emptiness of American political life today.

In the case of original liberalism, the matter can be simply and briefly described. Here the roots of the incapacity for governance lie mainly in a disbelief in government. This, as we have already noted, is not a disbelief in action. On the contrary, action on the part of industrial entrepreneurs and executives is regarded as the mainspring of prosperity and progress. But action by the government, apart from matters of foreign policy and defense, is assumed always to need special justification. The results have been so frequently and thoroughly discussed that here they need be only mentioned as they bear on the subject of this essay.

Original liberalism made a mockery of liberty by treating it as a legal formality and ignoring its actual context. It ignored first of all that liberty is not guaranteed by limited government. It is threatened by private powers as well as by government, and a government that acts to restrain those powers may widen liberty. This principle underlay much of the legislation undertaken by liberal governments during the first half of this century. Original liberalism also ignored the fact that liberty lacks significance if it is not enjoyed in a social environment in which values other than liberty, such as personal security and satisfying employment, make it possible to live with imagination and hope. History proves that these values, no less than liberty itself, often depend on governmental action. People who consistently adhered to the political negativism inherent in original liberalism could not conduct the affairs of a modern government. That people professing such negativism in fact have governed without disaster is because their actions do not have the ideological purity of their rhetoric. Fortunately, Ronald Reagan did not entirely mean it when he implied in his inaugural address that none of the internal problems we face could be solved by government but were all created by government.

We have already noted that reformist liberalism perceived these misconceptions and eliminated them from its own programs and actions but did this in a way that involved other ideological misconceptions. But in what way did those misconceptions involve an incapacity for governance?

To consider first the simpler part of a twofold answer: reformist liberals were overly casual about action. That many of the actions they undertook did not work, or entailed unforeseen consequences, is a commonplace of current social criticism, and the liberal answer—that some of the actions they undertook *did* work and that the actions that failed do not impose an imperative of inaction but of experimenting with alternatives—seems entirely adequate. Excluding original liberalism, what other answer could there be? To look for a sweeping new program of action, prescribing answers to all major problems, is simply to persist in ideological thinking. But the casual attitude toward action that was characteristic of reformist liberals had one consequence that liberals of a reformist persuasion mention now and then but leave ordinarily to be denounced by their antigovernmental opponents. That is bureaucracy.

Diatribes against the inefficiency and high-handedness of officials seem so much the hallmark of original liberalism that reformist liberals have had difficulty in recognizing that, however dubious the causes those diatribes served, on the whole they were true. It is not adequate to call the federal bureaucracy in America a fourth branch of the government. It is broadly true to say that it *is* the government and that it is merely influenced, but not controlled, by elected representatives, courts, pressure groups, and public opinion. It is neither efficient on the whole nor steadily and comprehensively under public supervision. It is obviously not incompatible with extensive liberties—not, at least, in the short run. But what are its long-range implications, not only for liberty but for other values, such as democracy. If liberal leaders could recognize that this is a question on which we must reflect, without entertaining the illusion that we can answer it by reducing government to nineteenth-century proportions, it would be a sign that supporters of liberty are breaking free of liberal ideology.

A second aspect of the political incapacity of reformist liberals calls for somewhat more extensive discussion. This comes from their assumption that all major values are harmonious. Anyone who accepts that assumption in all seriousness must become incapable of choosing for he cannot believe that any fundamental choices are necessary. But to govern, as has been said, is to choose. If all major values are compatible, then it is not necessary to choose. Practical judgments would have to be made but not moral judgments—judgments about the weight and relationship of values. This, I suggest, points to the sickness of contemporary reformist liberals. They are unable to think critically about values and the bearing of values on one another. And this is not merely because they lack experience. More basically, they lack the tragic sense of human existence which would enable them to realize that governance, at least in times like ours, requires meditation on values and the relations of values. It requires moral wisdom.

If my argument is sound, liberal leaders have been rendered superficial by ideology. They have been made insensitive to the perplexities arising from a situation without ideal possibilities. We may fail to see this because we think of ideological commitments as entailing a repressive insistence on moral or political absolutes. So far as they come from a consciousness of one all-embracing, imperative goal, as seen typically among revolutionaries, this is probably accurate. If the distinctive premise of ideological consciousness is the harmony of all values, however, then such consciousness in some circumstances might amount merely to a comfortable sense that no serious moral choices need to be made. In that case ideological commitments carry a moral indiscriminateness and an inability to resist demands from any quarter. This seems roughly to describe the state of reformist liberals. Such moral enervation can be seen in failures, some of which conservatives typically charge against them, some of which are spoken of mainly by radicals.

To begin with conservative concerns, one need not be a member of the Moral Majority to be disturbed by the spread of pornography, the use of abortion as a contraceptive, and the tendency to ignore the difficulties that homosexuality brings to social and personal life. Such practices and attitudes, typically defended on the basis of moral relativism, and existing against a background of family disintegration, can plausibly be seen as symptoms of the breakdown of civilization. It is no doubt foolish to invoke a simple moral prescription, call for a corresponding legal prohibition, and suppose that the issue has been answered. It is equally foolish, however, to dismiss the issue by invoking the principle of liberty, and few reformist liberals have done anything more than that. Few seem aware that one liberty might clash directly or indirectly with other liberties. This failure is particularly marked in view of the fact that such social issues belong less to original liberals, with their belief in liberty as the fountainhead of all values, than to reformist liberals, who have recognized some of the complexities involved in the realization of liberty. One does not expect, or even wish, to see a liberal presidential candidate base his campaign on a promise to wipe out pornography; but one may regret that liberal presidential candidates never seem thoughtful enough to be troubled by such a phenomenon as pornography.

Still looking at reformist liberals from the standpoint of conservative concerns, one may ask whether such liberals will ever have the strength and insight to resist the majority. Will they, for example, mindlessly support every possible extension of governmentally supported economic welfare? Leaders with a sense of the conflicts and paradoxes of history would see that widespread devotion to material welfare, even to material welfare distributed with meticulous fairness, is not apt to be favorable to liberty, at least not to liberty which encourages anything more than the expression of consumer preferences. It is one thing to take up the cause of material welfare when poverty and insecurity effectively nullify the liberty of large

numbers. It is another thing to pursue that cause with no regard for changing times or circumstances.

With reference to radical concerns, one of the most convincing accusations made against liberalism from the left is that
it lacks the ability to think in terms of the public interest. Even
reformist liberals often do little more than serve a conglom-
eration of particular, private interests. If values were as harmonious as they assume, there would be no harm in this. The
furtherance of every particular interest could be assumed to
be a furtherance of the public interest. Many elements of the
public interest, however, are not private interests at all—not
in the sense of being the interest of some particular group which
organizes in order to secure it; urban beauty may be cited as
an example. This fact has been often noted. What has not been
noted is that it is the ideological enervation of reformist liberals
which makes it difficult for them to deal with the fact. It is
usually charged that it is their individualism which blinds
them. No doubt their individualism is a factor. But no one can
begin to think about the public good who cannot ponder the
mutual bearing and relative importance of various values, and
it seems that most reformist liberals suffer from that incapacity.

I have already raised the question of whether reformist liberals have the strength in any circumstances to resist the majority. This question has a bearing not only on conservative
concerns but on typical radical concerns as well. During most
of the present century, responding to the wishes of the majority
has been roughly coincidental with doing what was necessary
to make liberty a reality for most people. This allowed, or even
encouraged, the assumption that all major values are in harmony. Now, however, it can be said that we are entering a
situation in which the majority enjoy the economic prerequisites of liberty and it is only minorities, constituted disproportionately of nonwhite races, who lack those prerequisites
and thus lack significant liberty. But the majority does not
demand—and may even resist—the rectification of that injustice. In short, two major values are now in conflict: majority rule
and minority rights. The minority rights in question are those
owed, but never yet granted, to racial, and therefore permanent, minorities. For anyone who acknowledges the conflict and

reflects on the values in contention, it is apt to become plain that priority in this case belongs to minority rights. But can people habituated to assuming that such conflicts do not exist make the necessary choice? It is easy to see that the future of a multiracial democracy may depend on whether they can.

This analysis of liberal weaknesses is obviously not intended to be comprehensive. Everything I have taken up has had to be dealt with summarily; otherwise, even the degree of comprehensiveness I have achieved would have been impossible. Also, there are many things I have scarcely touched on at all; liberal views of the proper ends of liberty, in societies so devoted to recreation and entertainment that everyone tends to think of liberty as merely a choice among possible pleasures, is an example. What I have tried to do is provide a sketch of a great cause that has been seriously, even fatally, weakened by optimistic oversimplifications of the kind to which our age, and perhaps our country, seems particularly susceptible. This sketch, it seems to me, might suggest ways of analyzing aspects of liberalism which have not been dealt with in this essay.

The view I have suggested clearly does not open the way to solutions. Indeed, what I have criticized in liberalism is the kind of thinking which supposes that where there is trouble there are always solutions. It might be said that the tragic view is that human life is inherently troubled and that many problems do not have solutions, whereas ideological thinking always depicts life as potentially untroubled. It is by their optimism that ideologies mobilize people for the application of solutions. The only adequate response to the present crisis of liberalism lies in a new—and also very old—way of looking at things. Such a response would not assure the future of liberalism but only, so to speak, its truthfulness—its fidelity to the somber vision of society and life that is presupposed in our very concern for liberty.

It goes without saying that it is uncertain whether any such alteration of attitude will occur. The ideological currents in history still seem strong and in America they are reinforced by our native optimism, worldliness, and taste for action. A tragic vision is not something a people can deliberately adopt, as they might a new process for refining steel.

One may ask, however, whether an altered attitude is even possible in the circumstances of modern life. One of my major themes has been that leaders are impelled to resort to ideological thinking in order to move multitudes of people to action. The presence of these multitudes on the political scene surely is, and in some form should be, permanent. And action will presumably always be necessary, even though the time may come when it will not be undertaken with the pragmatic assurance manifest among liberals in recent times. Is not ideology, then, a perdurable necessity of political life?

Probably it is. Political speech of tragic accent cannot reasonably be expected always to accord with historical necessity. But this is not the same as saying that ideology must be dominant in all situations. Surely history has possibilities more diverse than a simple ideological theory of action would allow for. It is striking that one of the greatest mass actions in American history, the mobilization of Northern manpower that preserved the Union during the Civil War, came about under a leader who did not rely on ideological appeals. Lincoln repeatedly spoke in tragic accents. He did this, of course, in exceptional circumstances. But his example must give pause to anyone inclined to conclude that ideological oversimplification is inseparable from democracy.

The possibilities of a common life free of ideology can be explored, however, only by leaders whose depth of vision impels them to speak truly even when it is risky to do so. American liberalism has rarely produced such leaders. Whether it is able to do so in the future may not decide our survival. But it may decide something almost as important, that is, our maturity. As a liberal nation, America is only as mature as its liberalism. Can we think that our taste for ideological oversimplification marks the adolescence of American liberalism and that a different and deeper age of liberty may be ahead of us?

NOTES

1. Fyodor Dostoevsky, *The Brothers Karamazov*, trans. Constance Garnett (New York: Modern Library), p. 262.

2. See, for example, Isaiah Berlin, *Four Essays on Liberty* (New York: Oxford University Press, 1969).

3. Helen Gurley Brown, *Having It All* (New York: Simon & Schuster/Linden, 1982).

Philip Abbott

III

Liberalism and Social Invention

In his conclusion to *Twilight of Authority* Robert Nisbet offers the concept of "social inventions" as both an approach to historical analysis and a solution to the restoration of authority in modern society. He argues that the concept of invention is improperly limited to technological change. There are cultural inventions (the epic poem, the tragedy and comedy, the novel, the essay, the painting, the fugue, the ballet, and the symphony) as well as social inventions. He contends that while we tend to call new forms "outcomes of 'cultural growth,'" this usage is an evasion. "Each is an invention. We invent forms of art just as we do mechanical things."[1]

Nisbet lists the following as social inventions: the walled town, the guild, the trade fair, the market place, the monastery, the university, the studio, the trading company, the mutual aid association, the labor union, and the economic corporation. He contends that the history of social organization is the history of the rise and spread of social inventions. According to Nisbet, there have been periods of relative dearth of such inventions and other periods of relative abundance. The Middle Ages were as rich in social organization as our own is in technological ones. The monastery, village community, manor, fief, guild, university, and parish are Nisbet's examples of medieval inventions. The Renaissance and Reformation were sterile, Nisbet tells us, as producers of new social forms. By contrast, the seventeenth century was another period of social invention with its creation of institutes and academies in the arts, letters, and sciences. The development of the "idea of the state from its absolutist to its popular form" captured the inventive minds of women and men but the nineteenth century, confronted with the challenge of industrialism, produced the mutual aid society in new forms, the consumers' and producers' cooperatives, the assurance societies, the labor unions, and the business corporations. In the United States there were waves of anarchist utopias and on the frontier, the storied logging and quilting bees. Nisbet sees the twentieth century as "singularly weak" in producing social inventions but he notes signs of inventiveness in the recrudescence of kinship, neighborhood, and local community as well as in the popularity of the contemporary commune.

I would like to examine Nisbet's concept of social invention in the context of American liberalism by asking the following questions: Can we identify liberal social inventions? Can social inventions rejuvenate American liberalism? What would these social inventions look like? But before I attempt to deal with these questions, I would like to propose some caveats and extensions to Nisbet's analysis.

My first concern is with possible objections to the analogy itself. One likely objection is that the concept of invention presents an individualized view of social change. No one really "invented" a trade union. The union "arose" as a result of changes in the nature of work and the market. We tend to think of the institutions mentioned by Nisbet as coming into existence in a different manner. A study of the labor union or the university will speak in terms of its rise, its growth, its development and its formation. More likely than not, such a study would tend to see the labor union as the culmination of or the vehicle for a social movement. But these approaches are analogical ones as well. They describe new institutions in terms of biological or mechanistic metaphors. The concept of invention as a description of new institutions highlights important aspects of social change that can otherwise be overlooked. The trade union as we now know it was not the only response available to industrialization. Even the character of the trade union itself (its internal organization and its goals) was the result of several possible options. In America Bill Haywood, Wyndam Mortimer, Samuel Gompers, and Walter Reuther all had different "inventions" in mind. The history of the trade union is in part a history of these competing personal visions. Some may not have been feasible; often it is difficult to say if they would have worked or not. Social inventions are indeed collective enterprises (although it may be a mistake to underestimate the role of individual contributions).

A related objection might emphasize the desirability of slow, experimental, and complex growth in institutions. The concept of invention suggests novelty and discovery and discontinuity, even gadgetry. In fact, Nisbet's willingness to use the concept shows his genius as a conservative. We are reminded of Edmund Burke's attack on the French revolutionaries: "By this unprincipled facility of changing the state as often, and as much, and in as many ways as their floating fancies or fashions, the whole chain and continuity of the commonwealth would be broken. No one generation could link with another."[2]

But the concept of invention is not totally inconsistent with an incremental view of historical change. The intricate machinery of the dial phone exchange is based upon thousands of smaller inventions. The relationship between the abacus, calculator, and computer reveals a sense of continuity. The first rocket used as a weapon in battle was used by defenders of a Chinese city in 1232. The history of representative government shows the same kind of process.

On the positive side, the concept of invention permits us to see the range of opportunities that are available in social life. As Nisbet remarks, we tend to see kinship systems as "some kind of evolutionary exfoliation of biological instincts." "We would do better," he says, "to conjure up a vision of some primitive Solon than of mere instinct in the fashioning of structures as ingeniously designed as clan, moiety, and tribe."[3] This is not to say that it is possible or desirable to invent whole new social orders, testing new inventions on unwilling and confused populations, as Burke warned against, or to believe that existing institutions ought to be casually replaced by new inventions, or to propose that such inventions do not need to be measured against basic human needs. The language of invention does suggest, however, that there may be circumstances in which invention is desirable, even necessary, and that the concept allows us to break away from certain historical impasses. The latter is, I think, the current case with American liberalism. But I do want to make a few additions to Nisbet's model before approaching this question.

Nisbet's approach suffers from two major defects as stated. First, he does not distinguish between kinds of social inventions. The market place and the local community are complexes of social institutions—the terms themselves are conceptual apparatuses for identifying whole networks of institutions. The quilting bee, on the other hand, is a social invention supporting a large set of institutions, the frontier settlement or town. Moreover, the business corporation (if indeed it is a *social* institution as Nisbet suggests), along with other inventions, transformed the market place into an institution of quite a different kind. Second, Nisbet seems to regard all institutions which are not direct agencies of the state as "social" inventions.

VARIETIES OF INVENTION

(1) Generative Inventions

There are some inventions that change our lives in momentous ways. They do so because they radically refashion our everyday existence and because they "generate" whole sets of supporting institutions. If we take a wide anthropological perspective, we can approach this category very broadly and identify the basic institutions of human culture as generative inventions. The origins of family forms and religions could, for instance, be seen as generative institutions whose inventors are lost in primitive history. In fact, Sigmund Freud approached the question of the origin of exogamy as a kind of invention. Freud posited the existence of a primal father who ruled over a horde of men and women, keeping all females to himself and driving away pubescent sons. One day the expelled sons joined forces, slew and ate the father, and thus put an end to the father horde. But without the primal father, the new brother clan was an ineffective organization. Every brother sought to be the father and was the other's rival among women. After many difficult experiences, the brothers invented the incest prohibition "through which they equally renounced the women whom they desired, and on account of whom they had removed the father in the first place." For Freud the family was a generative invention of tremendous consequence; it was the origin of "social organization, moral restrictions and religion."[4]

Fortunately for our purposes we need not accept Freud's account of the family as a generative institution, nor is it necessary for us here to establish the origins and nature of great inventions of human culture. These primal inventions may in fact be thought of as inventions in the broadest metaphorical sense, as human constructs, however gradually they emerged over time. Nisbet's examples of the walled town, the manor, and the university, while not of the significance of the invention of primordial family forms, are generative inventions. These inventions spawned new institutions themselves to become the major units in which successive generations would organize their lives. More recent examples would include the invention of a legislature, the complex of institutions that were to eventually surround it (different systems of election, representation, and rule-making), and the changes that it brought about throughout the whole society. Another might be the Marxist–Leninist invention of the Party. Here, events have been so rapid and so historically recent that it is possible to actually identify an inventor. In *What Is to Be Done?* Lenin conceived the Party to be the "vanguard of the revolutionary forces" and thus created what Hannah Arendt has called a secret society "established in broad daylight."[5] The Party, as invented by Lenin, altered the entire character of modern political systems. In societies in which it governed, the Party redefined the relationship between political action and social and governmental institutions. In countries in which the Party is out of power, it has created whole new forms of political activity (the front group is one).

(2) Supporting Inventions

Although it animates the vision of the revolutionary, the invention of generative institutions occurs rarely. Many inventions are designed to function as institutions that will support the goals of a broader existing institution. Nisbet's quilting bee met and helped sustain the needs of new towns and settlements by both providing a necessary service and fostering an arena for the development of sorority among transported women.[6] Other institutions also performed this task (house raisings, festivals, house warmings) and together they helped establish a particular kind of community. The loss of any one of these would not challenge the existence of the community among settlements.

A very different example is the invention of "mutual criticism" sessions in the American Oneida communes. The Oneidas were themselves attempting to invent a new generative institution, a family form based upon group marriage. In this community dyadic relationships were severely punished. At one point, couples were forbidden to spend the night with one another so that "private" conversation could be contained. Sexual partners were encouraged to confess their temptations to fall in love with a single individual.[7] These meetings were designed to reinforce community goals. In fact, the Oneida institution of mutual criticism was a new version of an invention widely used in social institutions. It bears some resemblance to the sacramental practice of confession in the Catholic Church and to self-criticism meetings in the Communist party. An individual is given some sort of immunity so that he or she may admit differences with the group and then is provided with the opportunity to return, suitably admonished, to the confines of the community. The "confession" is highly visible and structured in some communities and of course, much more subdued and informal in others. Nearly all work groups develop (or invent) the role of confidants as authority figures who represent the group's goals but who are neutral enough to hear complaints and transgressions. Within the family, the grandparent or aunt or uncle often performs this role. But the intention here is not to present a taxonomy of supportive inventions. The examples mentioned suggest that supporting inventions promote sociability and provide services in the context of group goals.

(3) Transitional Institutions

If some inventions create new forms and others sustain them, transitional institutions are inventions that alter both. They may themselves die out or they may continue as supporting institutions for new social forms.

Let me give two examples. Henri Pirenne in his *Economic and Social History of Medieval Europe* describes the trade fairs which began in the eleventh century and reached a peak in the thirteenth. Only the territorial prince had the right to found them. They were held along the great trade route which ran from Italy Provence to the coast of Flanders and lasted about six weeks. The trade fair provided a model for an economic system vastly different from that of the medieval town-based craft guilds. The canonical prohibition of usury was suspended as well as the fixing of maximum rates of interests. Merchants were protected by a special peace; all were under the protection of the territorial prince. "Guards of the fairs" (*custodes nundinarum*) maintained order and exercised a special jurisdiction at the fairs. Privileges were granted to attract the largest number of possible participants. One of the most common, aside from loans at interest, was a franchise which exempted fair merchants from the right of reprisal for crimes committed or debts contracted outside it, and from the right of escheat. Lawsuits were suspended as long as the fair lasted.

Pirenne notes that systems of international credit emerged from the fairs:

At every fair, after a preliminary period devoted to sales, there followed one of payments. These payments not only involved the clearing of debts contracted at the fair itself, but often settled credits contracted

at preceding fairs. From the twelfth century onwards this practice led
to the establishment of an organization of credit, in which we must
apparently seek the origin of bills of exchange.[8]

The fairs became an "embryonic clearing house." A variety of
factors led to the decline of the fair: the opposition by artisan
guilds, the plague, and the Hundred Years War. But Pirenne
contends that the trade fair opened up a new kind of economic
life in which use of correspondence and operations of credit
were employed by the new great commercial companies.

In the American context, the revival camp meeting has been
a major transitional invention. Ralph Gabriel has described
the camp meeting as the "unique American contribution to
Christianity."[9] During the Great Awakening even Benjamin
Franklin was impressed with the power of this new form:

The multitudes of all sects and denominations that attended were
enormous...it seemed as if all the world were growing religions, so
that one could not walk thro' the town in an evening without hearing
psalms sung in different families of every street.[10]

It is difficult to convey the impact of the camp meeting on
American religious and cultural beliefs. The camp meeting was
the key organizational structure of revivalism. Whole towns
signed documents of conversion and recommitment. James
Bradley Finley was an eyewitness to the Cane Ridge revival,
the largest and probably the most intense of the camp meetings:

We arrived upon the ground and here a scene presented itself to my
mind not only novel and unaccountable, but awful beyond description.
A vast crowd, supposed by some to have amounted to twenty-five
thousand, was collected together. The noise was like the roar of Ni-
agara. The vast sea of human beings seemed to be agitated as if by
storm. I counted seven ministers, all preaching at one time, some on
stumps, others in wagons....Some of the people were singing, others
praying, some crying for mercy in the most piteous accents, while
others were shouting vociferously.[11]

Like all successful inventions, the camp meeting was a response to various pressing and particular circumstances. In

New England, the temporary camp, constructed on the out-
skirts of town, provided a way for religious enthusiasts to seek
converts without directly challenging the established churches.
In other periods, it was used by existing churches to expand
and rededicate their membership. In the West, the camp meeting was an ideal form for reaching a large and sparsely pop-
ulated area. Moreover, the camp meeting, with its emphasis
on individual conversion, provided an avenue of recruitment
as the disestablishment of churches was becoming complete.
"Voluntarism" implied that all churches were potentially equal;
each had to support itself without compulsory taxation.

Perhaps the most historically significant impact of the Great
Revival was the democratization of American Protestantism.
Certainly part of this change arose from the nature of the camp
meeting itself. In order to repent and "come through," a par-
ticipant needed only to confess his sins and rededicate his life.
The camp meeting itself was based upon the principles of mass
conversion and mass admission. Charles Finney, one of the
most popular revivalists, claimed that "some of the best Christians of my acquaintance were convicted and converted in the
space of a few minutes."[12] This doctrinal change wreaked havoc
upon existing Protestant denominations. Schisms abounded and
all churches were forced to make accommodations.

There have been other transitional inventions in America:
the Chautauqua system, Francis Lowell's variant of the factory, the settlement house, tract housing, and the auto camp.[13]
Of course, one must be cautious in the identification of transitional institutions. These inventions do not always perform
the role expected of them. Nevertheless it is possible to find
new institutions that have redefined significant aspects of the
social order by altering institutional structures.

I have suggested that there are different kinds of inventions,
based upon their impact upon society. Is it possible to differ-
entiate broad categories of inventions? Nisbet includes as social
inventions all institutions that are not expressly technological
or cultural. Thus in his conception, the corporation, the credit
union, and the trade union are listed as social inventions along
with the commune, the quilting bee, and the university. Of
course, all institutions are social in a broad sense in that they

provide arenas of human interaction. The corporation provides for shared experiences that are unrelated to or even promote the goals of the institution. But the primary character of the corporation is economic. The same sort of assessment can be made about the Communist party. Undoubtedly, the Party performs a social function. In fact, members often remark that they suffer most from the loss of those social relationships made possible by the Party.[14] But the Party is primarily a political institution in both its goals and its activity.

Yet since all major institutions include social, economic, and political elements, it may be useful to attempt to sort them out. Take the extreme case of one of the most horrible inventions of the twentieth century, the concentration camp. The camp administration made every effort to systematically destroy social relationships. They punished those who shared food and shelter; they rewarded collaboration; they even forbade talking, the most basic form of social intercourse. On the whole, these efforts were successful. According to Bruno Bettelheim some inmates would reach the ultimate form of social withdrawal by becoming autistic. These prisoners would not eat or talk and responded to the environment in only robot-like fashion. However, Bettelheim does argue that even in this terrible world social relationships did exist. In fact, he contends that survival depended upon moments of social solidarity.[15]

The concentration camp in both the Fascist and the Stalinist variations was also an economic institution. But the use of slave labor, however important for Germany's war effort and the Soviet Union's economic development, was overshadowed by political goals. In Germany, the Wehrmacht competed unsuccessfully for freight space reserved for transportation of inmates. Inmates were recruited on political terms. The camps themselves were a significant agency of state policy.

Is it possible to identify institutions that are as fundamentally committed to social goals as others are to economic and political ones? Are there institutions whose basic function is the promotion of sociability leading to bonds of intimacy or friendship? This question is complicated by the fact that social institutions often find that they must develop political goals as defensive measures. One institution that fulfills this role is

the modern family. The economic basis of the family has obviously declined; today the family, with varying degrees of
success, functions primarily as a social agency. The complex of
institutions that constitute a neighborhood is another example
of a social institution. There are, of course, also institutions
whose functions are genuinely pluralistic in the sense that the
mix of economic, political, and social goals is relatively bal-
anced. Ideally the university functions in this manner as do
some religious groups and professional organizations. It is also
possible for institutions over time to alter their goals. Oneida,
for instance, dissolved into a more traditional form, the joint
stock company. The trade union may be moving toward assuming a more pluralistic character. For some time, writers have
predicted the transformation of the corporation into new forms.

IDEOLOGY AND INVENTION

We have identified inventions by function and type. Can we
match up inventions with ideologies, more specifically with the
great ideologies of the nineteenth and twentieth centuries, and
especially with liberalism? When we speak of technological
inventions, we tend to identify inventors. With proper quali-
fication, it is possible to say that Eli Whitney invented the
cotton gin, Samuel Colt, the revolver, and Thomas Edison, the
light bulb. Cultural inventions are a bit difficult in this regard,
but one could match up Samuel Richardson with the invention
of the novel, Horace Walpole with the Gothic, Arnold Schoen-
berg with atonal music, Louis Fuller, Ruth St. Dennis, and
Isadora Duncan with modern dance. Social and political inventors, as we have noted, are often hidden in history. We have
mentioned Lenin and the invention of the Party. Other examples might include the Founding Fathers and the invention
of the American system of representation, Luther and new
church forms, Bentham and the Panopticon.

One of the differences, however, between technological inventions and social, political, and economic ones is that in a
sense the latter must be invented again and again. New institutions are rediscovered and applied to new historical situations where they are readjusted and revised. Inventions which

were left unworked are sometimes seized upon by succeeding generations. In modern life, the task of bringing inventions into society is undertaken by ideological systems and movements. Ideologies propose new inventions; they mobilize support for these new institutions and when these campaigns are successful they refine and alter them. If we borrow from Karl Mannheim's analysis, ideological disputes involve the "reciprocal unmasking" of the utility of inventions. Liberals attack the Party as an institution of elite rule; Marxists defend it as an agency of economic and political change.

But let us begin to approach this matching up unsystematically in the same spirit as one would try to list the best modern baseball pitchers. One may have one's own preferences but boosterism is tempered by the principle of fairness. We have already listed the Party as Marxism's contribution to political invention. I can think of no more significant modern political invention. The Marxist conception of the Party is a generative institution. It bears little resemblance to "bourgeois" political parties. The Party created a new form of governmental organization. Not only has it redefined the relationship between voluntary association and the political system but it has produced an historically new elite. In fact, while it is certainly possible to imagine a Marxist society without the Party, such a development would represent so fundamental a change that Marxist regimes as we recognize them would cease to exist. Either some new generative institution(s) would need to take its place or the Party would have to be transformed into an organization resembling a liberal democratic model.

Although the concept of totalitarianism is not as compelling to scholars as it once was, the efforts of German and American writers to identify a new form of government (an invention, if you will) was in part the result of attempts to assess the significance of fascism and Stalinist Marxism. Theorists of totalitarianism lay the invention of the new form of a party to the experiences of both the Soviet Union and Germany. Certainly the NSDAP operated in ways similar to the Communist party. There are other practices common to both regimes: the system of terror and the camps, the systematic destruction and takeover of voluntary associations, and the militarization of society.

But I think the unique contribution of fascism, and of Nazism in particular, was the series of inventions that were themselves an outgrowth of the application of modern political and administrative techniques to racial ideology. Racism is, of course, not a new idea in Western thought nor is its systematic policy application. But the fascist invention in this regard involved the use of the concept in the context of the modern state. At the 1937 Reich party congress, Hitler announced that "Germany has experienced the great revolution...in national and racial hygiene which was undertaken for the first time on an organized basis in this country."[16] All this before the decree announcing the "final solution." This racial idea was incorporated into Nazi bureaucracy. Recruitment to the SS was governed by models of "Aryan" type. Bureaus within the SS were assigned functions relating to racial policy. The extermination camps were planned and administered by a section of the Economic and Administration Department of the SS. New inventions designed to deal with the race question blossomed. Each was in a sense a macabre transformation of modern institutions: eugenic institutes were created from the model of scientific research laboratories, sterilization wards from the model of the hospital, the Lebensborn programs from the model of foster homes, German farms in Poland (Volkstum) from the model of homesteading.

Democratic socialism is an especially syncretic ideology, one which is itself an inventive blend of Marxist and democratic elements. Its distinctive contribution to the invention of institutions is, I think, that complex of institutions we refer to as the welfare state. Democratic socialists have advocated the use of the legislature as the wellspring for a series of institutional inventions: public corporations, national health insurance, social security, day care, and more recently the ombudsman. The alliance between party, legislature, administrative agency, and voluntary association (trade unions and allied groups) provides the conditions for inventions in democratic socialistic systems. These inventions have been widely accepted and adapted by both liberal and Marxist regimes. In fact, one of the unique features of the welfare state as an invention has been its ability through creation of a political-administrative infrastructure, to establish a kind of permanent laboratory or engine of invention. This results from two factors: the desire on the part of the welfare state apparatchiki to extend their hegemony over society and the stresses of industrial societies which create demands for solutions to economic problems. This special feature of the welfare state angers its opponents from the left and the right. It is intriguing that the commitment to the welfare state is a tentative one for many democratic socialists. It is something which must be "transformed" or "surpassed" since it seems so capable of absorbing stress through inventive reform.[17] The right, of course, focuses upon the welfare state's expansive nature. When forces which might obstruct this institutional structure of invention are weak or do not exist, the welfare state, for good or bad, assumes its most complete inventive character. Thus one finds in Sweden vigorous attempts to develop new inventions. New programs in female equality are one example; the proposed wage funds as a step toward workers' control is another. From the opposite perspective, in Marxist regimes in which the Party has been weakened, the welfare state apparatus develops inventions that take on a liberal character. Hungary's unique approach to family policy, lengthy extended paid leaves for mothers rather than day care, is an example of this sort of development.

What is the contribution of liberal ideology to political, economic, and social invention? Certainly liberals in the United States have made a contribution to the invention of the welfare state. But these efforts have often been pushed reluctantly and with peculiar emphasis. For many liberals the welfare state deserves support only as a kind of Rousseauean second or third choice. For instance, Richard Hofstadter has argued that the American Progressives, even in their role as the first architects of the welfare state, were "trying to keep the benefits of the emerging organization of life and yet retain the scheme of individualistic values that this organization was destroying."[18]

I think that liberalism is responsible for mobilizing support for—if not more directly inventing—two great generative inventions of the modern age. One is the invention of the constitution. The other is the market economy. As I noted earlier in this essay, generative institutions often represent a series of inventions. This is certainly the case with the constitution and the market. The idea of a constitutional system has been advanced and developed by generations of liberals. All the variations of the conception of constitutional government—as rule of law, as limited power, and as express and written authority— were the result of a whole pantheon of liberal inventors extending from the British Commonwealthmen to Locke and Montesquieu, to Jefferson, Madison, to Constant and Tocqueville, and to Dahl. In each of these writers, the idea of constitutional government is redefined and reinvented, often with new supporting structures.

Again, it is necessary to note that liberalism is not the only defender of constitutional government. Nevertheless, liberalism has held this invention so dearly that it is largely responsible for the continued existence and development of constitutional government. The constitution as a political institution operates in only a limited number of nation-states. But its potential as a generative institution still exists.

To say that liberalism invented the modern market economy is a more complicated statement. The changes that eventually created the market economy—the breakdown of certain structures such as the guild and commons and the invention of new ones such as finance capital and the factory—were in a large part instituted or supported by liberal writers. Locke, Smith, Bentham, and James Mill certainly anticipated or nurtured or advocated the market economy. Many of them offered inventions of their own. We do not have the space to trace the relationship between liberalism and the market but it is worth noting that liberals have not always been the doting parents of their own invention. They have worried about the social and political consequences of a market economy. Some have not supported its more recent development. As Irvin Kristol notes, while the Founding Fathers "*intended* this nation to be capitalist and regarded it as the *only* set of economic arrangements consistent with the liberal democracy they had established," the large publicly owned corporation would have "troubled and puzzled them."[19] The corporation puzzles and troubles Kristol himself. But he concludes (as many liberals have done) that "we frequently find ourselves defending specific concentrations of power, about which we might otherwise have the most mixed feelings, on the grounds that they contribute to a general diffusion of power, a diffusion which creates the 'space' in which individual liberty can survive and prosper."[20] Robert Dahl, the modern American authority on pluralism, takes a less sanguine view. He has argued that the corporation in its present form "cannot be justified."[21]

In any case, the market economy (however modified or even transformed by both the corporation and the welfare state) continues to exercise a fascination for many liberals. In fact, several recent works by American liberals argue in different ways that the market economy must be supported precisely because it is itself such a dynamic inventive system.[22]

LIBERALISM AND SOCIAL INVENTION

If we look then at the great ideologies of the modern era we find one outstanding feature. The major inventions that we have identified (the Party, racial bureaucracy, the welfare state, the constitution, and the market) are all primarily political or economic inventions. That this condition is not unique to liberalism is not an acceptable reason for complacency. The relative scarcity of new social inventions in the context of modern liberalism creates special problems which threaten its very future.

Let me take a moment to attempt to show why this is so. Liberals have invented and supported two extremely powerful institutions. Constitutional government and a market economy are generative institutions of such capacity for expansion that they overwhelm the social content of every institution they encounter. Many liberals have, of course, argued precisely the opposite. Limited government and allocation of economic resources by a market will produce a free and relatively equal society. Both institutions will reinforce one another and create vast areas of social space that will allow individuals to pursue varied life plans. This, in essence, was J. S. Mill's argument in *On Liberty*, the most eloquent and moving statement of modern liberalism. For some time now individuals have denied the validity of this proposition. Where, they ask, is freedom in repression and equality in poverty? Many liberals have to some degree accepted these accusations and attempted to provide corrective institutions. The principles of constitutionalism have thus been extended to include the protection of minorities, and the market has mechanisms built into it to include provision for entitlements and public goods. Radicals have replied that such measures are inadequate. But the real significance of this activity is the preoccupation with political and economic mechanisms themselves. There is no confidence that social institutions can be a useful connective to the problems of liberalism. Liberals themselves generally support this critique.

Thus on the one hand, social institutions must submit to the scrutiny of constitutional control and on the other, their functions are constantly being absorbed by the forces of the market economy. Liberalism has produced a peculiar amalgam of Lockean and Hobbesian individuals. In politics we are anxious to locate the power quotient in all institutions and to control it by contract. In the economic sphere we are utility maximizers. Either—and often both—of these perspectives infects our approach to social institutions. Liberalism approaches social institutions with the eye of the constitutional or corporate lawyer.

Even the great tradition of liberal pluralism has pursued this approach. Tocqueville saw that liberal society produced enormous numbers of social groups. But he also saw that associational activity in America had a different character from that of European societies. Association rose on other than "natural" sentiments. Liberal societies produced groups that lacked permanence and stability. Yet Tocqueville argued that this basis of group formation was better than none at all. He posited the principle of enlightened self-interest as the motivation for social institutions in America. Such activity might not "inspire great sacrifices" nor "make a man virtuous" but it would create "orderly, temperate, moderate, carefree and self-controlled citizens."[23]

Modern pluralists have ignored Tocqueville's famous warning that supplemented his analysis. "I see a multitude of men," he prophesied, "alike and equal, constantly circling in pursuit of petty and banal pleasures with which they glut their souls.... Over this kind of man stands an immense, protective power. . .absolute, thoughtful of detail, orderly, provident and gentle."[24] These pluralists from Madison to Truman and even Dahl have written a great deal about social groups but they have invariably treated them as politico-economic entities. Madison saw them as factions bent upon the seizure of power through "domestic convulsion" and "schemes of oppresssion." David Truman portrayed all groups as temporary and over-lapping collections of interests. Even the category of citizenship was presented as some vast "consumer group."[25] Robert Dahl, the most imaginative and reflective of modern American pluralists, continues to see group membership in terms of marginal utility. Institutional affiliation will continue until rational self-interest requires a calculation that "the loss would exceed the gain."[26]

With social institutions viewed in this manner, it is natural that they will be treated to increasing political control and domination by economic incentive. If the theory of the firm is the basis for our conception of social groups, then groups will use this as the basis for recruitment and goals, as will the political system for regulation and supervision. Such a state of affairs does create a climate for invention, but it is a climate which fosters the invention of institutions of political and economic control. It is no accident that so many of our institutions today look and behave alike. Hospitals, schools, prisons, professional organizations, churches, newspapers, and universities not only see the same methods of institutional defense and expansion but are increasingly internally organized on the same basis. When one walks into the lobby of any of these institutions, one at first finds them indistinguishable. There is an information desk, a waiting alcove, and clearly identified entrances and exits. The lobby is remarkably quiet. Staff walk through quickly, information officers speak in hushed tones, entrants sit silently. If one proceeds further, he or she will continue to see major similarities. One confronts a receptionist for identification and "facilitation" purposes. Then one is assigned a staff officer, and, depending upon whether one is a visitor or a member, the procedure of further identification, examination, and record-keeping and processing continues.

These institutional features are, of course, the result of bureaucratization and professionalization, characteristics, one would be reminded, of all modern organization. But on another level, these characteristics reflect adaptions to a universe dominated by political and economic perspectives. Only a pseudo-sociability is encouraged in these settings. Entrants are frequently addressed by first name. The structure itself encourages economic and political behavior on the part of the member or visitor. Entrants either move through the institution as an object, quietly responding to the next request for information (each in itself rational and efficient) or challenge the system with political or economic retaliation. No other alternatives are available.

Despite this domination of the political and economic in liberal societies, there are possibilities for a social renewal. For the very propositions which have created the conditions we have just described still hold out the opportunity for a different set of developments. A liberal society, even with its "social space" contracted and withered by the hegemony of political and economic organization, continues to provide the potentiality for social invention.

Let me conclude this essay by focusing upon ways in which the conditions for social invention can be established. First, it must be recognized that, more than in previous periods in the history of American liberalism, social space must be won. It must be wrestled and torn away from economic and political institutions. New supporting inventions must be invented for the remaining social institutions that now exist. In other instances, transitional and even generative inventions are necessary to replace or significantly alter existing institutions.

Those periods in which social inventions proliferated in America were the result of different circumstances. The "inventive communities" in America—colonial settlements, the frontier, the town, the commune—created social inventions as adaptive measures to create social space in a relative vacuum. As Michael Zuckerman has illustrated so well in his *Peaceable Kingdoms*, the New England town meeting was as much an agency of sociability as of politics.[27] Even when one moves from the discipline of rural Massachusetts communities to the much more fluid and tolerant Quaker Philadelphia, one finds different

kinds of concerted efforts to create a social order through invention. America, or the world, has no greater inventor than
Benjamin Franklin. His contributions to social inventions such
as the library, hospital, university, and even the Junto itself,
reveal a sense of social utility applied to the creating of a more
hospitable urban environment. We have discussed some of the
social inventions of the frontier settlements. The communes,
those antiliberal institutions which thrived so in liberal societies, used the principles of toleration and the geographic ex-
panse of America to create new social foundings. The American
small town, before its economic disintegration, successfully created inventions like the town lecture, "self-improvement societies," and the Sunday School library to fuse educational and
social objectives. The American system of public education itself, from the schoolhouse to the private college to the land
grant university, was created or supported by local communities. In many cases these institutions became agencies of
political reform. In urban centers where new immigrants were
set adrift in a strange land, neighborhoods which reflected the
character of several cultures were created through newspapers,
clubs, and extended family networks.

But to a greater or lesser degree in each of these cases, social
inventions arose in the absence of existing dominating political
and economic structures. Social space is now increasingly filled
up or enclosed. The case of the family as a social institution is
a good example. In many ways the modern family is itself a
liberal invention. The conception of a family which is nuclear,
child-centered, and based upon an emotional and erotic relationship between relatively equal spouses was based upon the
pedagogy of liberals or the result of political and economic
changes advocated by liberals. Today that version of the family
is undergoing a major transformation. The new average American family is quite small (household size was 2.73 in 1981)
and increasingly it is headed by a single parent. The shrinkage
in family size itself limits the character of social relationships.
In some ways, this feature is counteracted by the creation of
new forms of extended families (divorced parents, then new
partners and children). Johnny is now said to have benefited
from divorce. He now has a "new" mom or dad and "new"

brothers or sisters. But there is no question that the character of familial social relationships has been altered. Moreover, the entry by women into the work force, the rise of marriage contracts, and the increase in rates of illegitimacy suggest that the family is ceasing to function as a social institution. The problem is not, as some critics argue, the result of the flight of working women from the home. The problem, at least in part, lies in the nature of work itself in modern society. Work is assigned individually, physically away from the home, and according to a precise schedule. Yet the demands of liberal reform do not seek to recover this social element in family life but seek rather to replace it with new supporting political and economic institutions such as the public or employee day-care center or expanded school programs. In a recent study of family policy reform, the authors remind us that future policy must be premised upon full labor participation regardless of sex and that "society does not owe an equal standard of living to those that prefer to trade the home contributions of one partner against income from work."[28]

One would hope that liberals would examine the consequences of this new absorption of both adults and children by new institutions. An example of one such approach is an article by Elizabeth Jones and Elizabeth Prescott.[29] They have focused their concern over the impact of adult role model behavior in day-care centers. Day-care staff frequently change jobs within the system which naturally is designed to accommodate change: "A bureaucracy—and most day care is becoming bureaucratic in design—is organized to promote efficient task accomplishment through clear definition of roles, so that individuals can be replaced without interrupting the task." Competent care is, of course, assured but "when a day-care giver moves, she says goodbye. And the child mourns—or learns not to care." If one couples this behavior with the high divorce rates of the new American family, there is cause for a complete evaluation of the bureaucratic alternative to child-rearing. Jones and Prescott note that one recurrent finding of day-care studies is that children in day care appear to be more oriented to peers than to adults. They noted that "peers are able to give children a sense of the present—but not of the future."[30] Any alternative to day care must include the creation of "a coherent sense of community, in which adults can act with purpose and commitment, and children can absorb and internalize this mode of being in the world."

The creation of new communities with "purpose and commitment" should indeed form the future agenda of liberalism. In the case of family policy the most immediate task must include the creation of social space itself through attempts to restrict the economic demands placed upon employees. One such proposal has been offered by Z. I. Giraldo who has recommended borrowed paid time for parents with young children.[31] We may find that the expansion of social space itself will reveal imminent social structures. For example, Alice Collins and Diane Pancoast have argued that in every human setting there exist "natural helping networks," linkages among relatives, friends, and acquaintances. These networks revolve around a "central figure," "natural neighbor," or gatekeeper who "acts as an exchange agent or a match-maker for needs and resources, and also offers direct advice, support, and practical help to members of a network."[32] They contend that such social networks are being rediscovered and studied and that they hold real promise for positive intervention in human problems on a large scale at a feasible cost. The resuscitation of these networks (which these writers admit are often unknown to health and service professionals) could provide a condition for social invention.

The second condition involves a basic alteration in liberal philosophy itself. Liberals can be identified by their acceptance of two sets of beliefs. One contains a utopian premise. It celebrates the desirability of the existence of a plurality of forms of the good life individually accepted. The other is scientific in the sense that it captures a central feature of existing societies. It involves the acceptance of permanent human conflict. The adherence to both beliefs is, as I have analyzed elsewhere, unique to liberalism.[33] But this set of beliefs creates enormously powerful pressures on the part of liberals to find a resolution. The liberal individual must be given opportunities to select the best life plan suitable to him or her but this plan will conflict with those chosen by others. No writer saw this dilemma more clearly than Thomas Hobbes. His resolution, a Leviathan state, in which each individual voluntarily sees that he or she must submit to a far-reaching centralized political authority, stands as an archetypical warning to liberals. Other writers have embraced the market for the same reasons. In the market society each individual is free to select his own conception of the good life. Conflict is channeled into productive competition.

We can see then that when the liberal approaches the question of social groups, he or she assumes an ambivalent position. A wide variety of such groups is desirable since such a condition allows for each person to select his/her own life plan. But a pluralist society produces conflict; some moral settlement must be reached. Moreover, social groups can be aggressive and over-whelming in their demands for loyalty. They must be super-vised so that rights of egress can be assured. Groups which threaten to close off full and complete individuality must be regulated or banned. What emerges are groups which require only limited, temporary, and overlapping allegiance. In a recent book Lewis Coser complains about the existence of "greedy organizations," groups which deny the individual's uniqueness. He includes the Catholic Church and the family as greedy institutions.[34] As a result, of course, liberals are left only with economic and political incentives to guarantee both their scientific and their utopian premises.

One should not expect nor should one hope that liberalism will alter its basic beliefs. These beliefs admit of a great number of variations, some of which are historically untried. Nor should one expect that liberalism will not always have a preference for social institutions that are loosely joined and limited in scope. But liberals must develop a philosophy that is truly social. They must learn that a world that has an expanded social element is not one which restricts individual vision and fosters what John Stuart Mill called "ape-like imitation." A world rich in sociability need not be a static and insulated place as so many conservatives implicitly assume. On the contrary, it can be a world of proliferating social inventions, a world

which sees what Jean Bethke Elshtain has called a "redemp-
tion of everyday life,"[35] a world which truly encourages a utopian spirit of association.

NOTES

1. Robert Nisbet, *The Twilight of Authority* (New York, 1975),
p. 279.
2. Edmund Burke, "Reflections on the French Revolution," in *The
Collected Works of Edmund Burke*, vol. II (London, 1854), p. 366.
3. Nisbet, *Twilight of Authority*, p. 280.
4. Sigmund Freud, *Totem and Taboo* (New York, 1918), p. 182.
5. Hannah Arendt, *The Origins of Totalitarianism* (New York,
1951), p. 376. On the significance of the personal contribution of Lenin
to this new party form, see Adam Ulam's account, *The Bolsheviks*
(New York, 1965), pp. 160–218.
6. It should be noted that, as is the case with many supporting
inventions, the quilting bee also reveals an element of antagonism to
general cultural norms. These meetings were also an arena in which
opposition to patriarchal attitudes were developed and sharpened. The
bee then also contained an embryonic alternative community beneath
its supporting layer. This feature is subtly revealed in chapters on
quilting in two nineteenth-century novels, Harriet Beecher Stowe's
The Minister's Wooing and Eliza Culvert Hall's *Aunt Jane of Kentucky*.
7. Charles Nordhoff attended a mutual criticism session at Oneida
and provides a vivid verbatim account in his book *The Communistic
Society of the United States* (New York, 1961), p. 293.
8. Henri Pirenne, *Economic and Social History of Medieval Europe*
(New York, 1937), p. 102.
9. Ralph Gabriel, *The Course of American Democratic Thought*
(New York, 1940), p. 32.
10. Benjamin Franklin, *Autobiography and Other Writings*, ed.
Russel B. Nye (Boston, 1958), p. 97.
11. James Bradley Finley, *Autobiography* (Cincinnati, 1858), p. 166.
12. Charles G. Finney, *Lectures on Revivals of Religion* (New York,
1835), p. 189.
13. For a fascinating account of one such recent transitional invention, the professional reform organization, see Joseph H. Helfgot's
*Professional Reforming: Mobilization for Youth and the Failure of
Social Science* (New York, 1981).
14. There are many treatments of this phenomenon. For me, the
most moving is Richard Wright's *American Hunger* (New York, 1944).

Also revealing is Vivian Gornick's *The Romance of American Communism* (New York, 1977).

15. Bruno Bettelheim, "Reflections: Surviving," *The New Yorker* (August 2, 1976), pp. 31–52.

16. Cited in Ernest Nolte, *Three Faces of Fascism* (New York, 1963), p. 382.

17. See Michael Walzer, *Radical Principles* (New York, 1980) and Michael Harrington, *The Twilight of Capitalism* (New York, 1976).

18. Richard Hofstadter, *The Age of Reform* (New York, 1955), p. 217.

19. Irving Kristol, "On Corporate Capitalism in America," in *The American Commonwealth: 1976*, ed. Nathan Glazer and Irving Kristol (New York, 1976), p. 125.

20. Ibid., p. 140.

21. Robert Dahl, *After the Revolution* (New Haven, 1970), p. 116.

22. Robert Nozick, *Anarchy, State and Utopia* (New York, 1974); Michael Novak, *The Spirit of Democratic Capitalism* (New York, 1982); George Gilder, *Wealth and Poverty* (New York, 1981).

23. Alexis de Tocqueville, *Democracy in America*, ed. J. P. Mayer (Garden City, N.Y., 1969), p. 507.

24. Ibid., pp. 691–92.

25. David Truman, *The Governmental Process* (New York, 1951), pp. 51–52.

26. Dahl, *After the Revolution*, p. 12.

27. Michael Zuckerman, *Peaceable Kingdoms* (New York, 1970). More recently Jane J. Mansbridge has brilliantly reconstructed a general model of friendship from the contemporary town meeting in her *Beyond Adversary Democracy* (New York, 1980).

28. Sheila B. Kamerman and Alfred J. Kahn, *Child Care, Family Benefits and Working Parents* (New York, 1981), p. 251.

29. Elizabeth Jones and Elizabeth Prescott, "Day Care: Short or Long Term Solution?" *The Annals of the American Academy of Political and Social Science* (May 1982), p. 95.

30. Ibid.

31. Z. I. Giraldo, *Public Policy and the Family* (New York, 1980).

32. Alice H. Collins and Diane L. Pancoast, *National Helping Networks* (Washington, D.C., 1976), p. 18.

33. See my *Furious Fancies: American Political Thought in the Post-Liberal Era* (Westport, Conn., 1980).

34. Lewis Coser, *Greedy Institutions: Patterns of Undivided Commitment* (New York, 1974).

35. Jean Bethke Elshtain, *Public Man, Private Woman* (Princeton, N.J., 1981), p. 335.

Jean Bethke Elshtain

IV

The Liberal Captivity of Feminism: A Critical Appraisal of (Some) Feminist Answers

A *picture* held us captive. And we could not get outside it, for it lay in our language and language seemed to repeat it to us inexorably.

Wittgenstein, *Philosophical Investigations*

I propose to look at "the obvious."* It is precisely the beliefs, principles, and practices that appear to us self-evident that most require explanation. Specifically, I intend to step outside the frame of a powerful picture—ultra-liberalism[1]—in order to examine critically its interlocked presuppositions, stated and submerged. I shall argue that the dominant forms of contemporary American feminism are captive to this ultra-liberalism, sharing with it general doctrines and important philosphical commitments. If I am correct, the implication is simply this: the organized forces of feminism frequently affirm at a deep level central features of a society feminists claim, explicitly, to reject or to challenge. My aim in this essay is not demolition

---

*I do not claim that this critique exhausts the entire range of feminist debate; rather, what I aim to do is to expose the unstated assumptions that help to constitute American feminist theory in its primary forms of expression.

for its own sake. Instead, I hope, first, to open up some conceptual and political space for the consideration of counterideals to ultra-liberalism. Second, by showing the ways in which the feminism I critique may unwittingly reinforce undemocratic tendencies in a liberal society, I aim to challenge us feminists to grow more reflective about our enterprise and to consider democratic alternatives to entrenched liberalism.

None of us, to be sure, can shed altogether her cultural skin, but we can become more reflective about what makes our social and political order what it is. We can reconceive relations and practices, perhaps to reveal a richness and ambiguity received formulae concealed. One aim of the social theory I embrace—an interpretive, desimplifying enterprise—is to work toward a more complete description of which is really going on, of how things are with us. This may be done, or attempted, in a number of ways. One might expose certain practices and doctrines as self-defeating or, alternatively, rescue other practices and ideals as vital to a cherished vision of the human community. No doubt one cannot require of political activists that they be self-critical and reflective about their enterprise from its inception—given the heat of battle, the demand for solidarity, the urgency to get results. So they proceed: "We hold these truths to be self-evident." Self-evident truths are often bulwarks, common rallying points and powerful symbolic markers. But they may rapidly become a liability, locking social participants into moribund usages that seriously misdescribe their project and point them down false paths to liberation or wisdom. Such seems to me the story of the dominant feminism and the doctrine of ultra-liberalism. But before I tell this tale, I must lodge the usual number of cowardly caveats.

I recognize that feminism cannot be pinned down and held in place with a single theoretical skewer. I explore feminism's most prevalent forms of expression—this is what I have in mind when I refer to the "organized forces" of feminism. My reference point, however, is not simply or only feminism that describes itself as "liberal" but modes of feminist thought that proclaim themselves more radical. Upon closer examination one often uncovers an important, not trivial, convergence of "non" or "anti" liberals with their liberal counterparts to the extent that each is built upon the dominant liberal *episteme*. That is, the presuppositions and rules they share may be more important than their proclaimed differences.[2] This will become clearer as the essay takes shape.

The reigning ultra-liberal *episteme* cannot be "stretched" to cover every form of feminist association and identity. One finds separatist feminists preaching withdrawal from a wider surround which they declare tainted. Religious feminist women embrace images of self and other that diverge significantly from ultra-liberal construals. Antimilitarist feminists challenge the state. Feminist consciousness-raising embraces as expressivist vision of the language-using self and celebrates human connections in a way that does not mesh tidily with the dominant *episteme*. And so on.

I do not share the view of some radical critics who proclaim our liberal inheritance a rotten deal through and through. By distinguishing ultra-liberalism from liberalism as such, I avoid painting a monochrome picture. Although I believe sources for political renewal are present within liberalism in its democratic and participatory "moments," I also find these options under relentless pressure to succumb to the combined force of those beliefs, practices, and commitments I aim to indict. This is a worry. If I am even partially correct, it means that the dominant liberalism, its priorities and doctrines deployed increasingly as vehicles and rationalizations for newer modes of social control, has become self-defeating. Inside the picture, one is struck with more of what has helped to sicken us in the first place: final rationalization and disenchantment of all aspects of social life; deeper dependency of the self on antidemocratic bureaucracies and social engineering elites; a more complete stripping away of the last vestiges of personal authority (construed as domination), traditional identities (construed as irrational and backward), and so on. The entanglement of feminism with this liberal project, and its possible derailment, is a feature of social order, at this very moment, that tends to go unmarked, perhaps unthought.

THE ATOMIST TURN IN POLITICAL DISCOURSE

What makes ultra-liberalism run? The foundational motor that moves the system is a particular notion of the self. That self helps to make ultra-liberalism what it, complicatedly is, including its characteristic construal of social reality. There is no single, shared understanding of self that grounds all forms of liberal theorizing. The transcendental subject of Kant's deontological liberalism, for example, is a being at odds with the prudential calculator of Bentham's utilitarianism. Ultra-liberalism's vision of self flows from seventeenth-century atomist discourse, a doctrine linked to the names of Hobbes and, less tightly, Locke. Atomism posits a self as given, prior to any social order—ahistorical, unsituated, a bearer of abstract rights, an untrammeled chooser in whose choices lies its freedom and autonomy.

One ineliminable feature of atomism, then, "is an affirmation of what we could call the primacy of rights."[3] Although atomism ascribes primacy to rights, it denies the same status to any principle of belonging or obligation. Primacy of rights has been one of the important formative influences on the political consciousness of the West. We remain so deeply immersed in this universe of discourse that most of us most of the time unthinkingly grant individual rights automatic force. Atomism makes this doctrine of primacy plausible by insisting on the "self-sufficiency of man alone or, if you prefer, of the individual."[4] Closely linked to right's primacy is the central importance atomists attach to freedom understood, as I noted, as "freedom to choose one's own mode of life,"[5] to constitute and choose values for oneself. In making freedom of choice an absolute, atomism "exalts choice as a human capacity. It carries with it the demand that we become beings capable of choice, that we rise to the level of self-consciousness and autonomy where we can exercise choice, that we not remain mired through fear, sloth, ignorance, or superstition in some code imposed by tradition, society, or fate which tells us how we should dispose of what belongs to us."[6] Solidified by market images of "sovereign choice," the atomist self was pitted with great success against older, "unchosen" constraints.

This atomist picture of freedom remains so deeply entrenched that we tend to see the "natural" condition or "end" of human beings as one of self-sufficiency (though deep down we probably know better). Atomism's vision of self, its absolutizing of choice, and its celebration of radical autonomy all cast suspicion on times of reciprocal obligation or mutual interdependence and help to erode the traditional bases of personal authority in family and polity alike. Feminists make their indebtedness to atomist construals powerfully manifest when they proclaim choice an absolute, granting the "right to choose" *prima facie* force. The likely result is that any perceived constraint or chastening of individual choice is suspect and will be assessed from the standpoint of the atomist standard. There is another outcome. Once choice is absolutized, important and troubling questions that arise as one evaluates the writ over which individual right and social obligation, respectively, should run are blanked out of existence. One simply gives over everything, or nearly so, to the individualist pole in advance. Embracing "free choice" and primacy of rights as self-evident truths and their liberal birthright, the feminist thinkers I shall criticize have been somewhat uncritical about their own theoretical commitments. This makes sense, of course, for, as the daughters of liberal society, they *have* been deprived of freedom.

I shall move from this plane of abstract principle to the particulars of feminism's atomistic turn by getting inside dominant, or widespread, feminist images of *the body, the family*, and *the citizen*. I hope to show the ways in which each image is entangled in the conceptual grid of ultra-liberal discourse, subject to identical challenges and derailments.

THE BODY AS ALIEN "OTHER"

The female body has been constituted in feminist discourse as political battleground, the locus of a struggle for control. To appreciate the *terms* of feminist description and evaluation of the body, one must first look back at liberalism's historic suspicion of the body and its desires. Classical liberalism valorized a public world in which adult (male) persons, stripped of particular passion, shared an identical commitment to prudential reasons. The arbitrariness of desire was consigned to the nonpublic sphere; it lay outside the official writ of the liberal *episteme*. Yet this potentially chaotic and uncontrollable desire was required to hold liberal rationalism intact, serving as its mirror opposite. Keeping the beasts in their place milling about inside the private corral, liberals aimed to liberate men from a double subjection: to the rule of the traditional patriarch and to privatized passion.[7]

John Stuart Mill accepted this bifurcation, contrasting Reason with the abyss of Instinct, "the worse rather than the better parts of human nature."[8] The rational man, striving for an "apotheosis of Reason" must reject utterly the "idolatry" of "Instinct," an idolatry "infinitely more degrading than any others...."[9] When relations between men and women are lifted up to the realm of Reason, Mill declares, then and only then will they be free from the taint of unscrupulous desire. The body itself must come under the sway of wider social force of liberal rationalization and its ethos, one that dictated setting to one side, or stripping away, all distinctions and specific identities that situate us and define us as particular beings rather than universal, abstract, moral agents. And it is true that to make good on Mill's version of the liberal promise, men and women must abstract *from* their sexual identities, eschew "arbitrary passions," and only then usher in the halcyon world of sex equality.[10]

Occlusion and denial of the body remains a dominant thread in modern feminist discourse. Mill's insouciance gives way to Beauvoir's disdain of female embodiment. Her animus, though extreme, makes discursive sense for Sartrean existentialism; her frame of analysis, is in part a variant on liberal doctrine. Beauvoir's excoriation of the female body as "inessential," a prefixed abyss that condemns women to a nether world of unfreedom (Immanence), bearing the stigma, "victim of the species," is familiar to feminist thinkers and social theorists. Beauvoir constitutes the body as an alien "Other," the enemy of the "free project" of Transcendence. The woman is, by definition, an alienated being given her biological capacity to bear a child. Menstruation, childbirth, nursing—all are portrayed as a chamber of smelly, painful bodily horrors.[11] Sharing a central marker of liberal atomism, Beauvoir splits the rational self from its unfree embodiment.

Beauvoir helped to set the terms for dualist feminism's "somatophobia," fear of the body. This repudiation of embodiment reached its apogee in Shulamith Firestone's 1972 tract, her indebtedness to Beauvoir made explicit, which locates the oppression of women *in nature*: we are oppressed because we are embodied. Swallowing whole a depiction of nature as the unfree, unthought—lacking sentience and meaning—Firestone embraces atomism, technocratic hubris, domination of nature, scientific engineering, scientific rationality, and a rather muddled notion of aesthetics as her feminist utopia. She situates the most problematic, potentially undemocratic features of liberal capitalism's historic trajectory in the heart of her feminist project.

One might evade the matters at stake here by claiming, as is often done, that the texts I here criticize are "old"; that no one takes Firestone seriously; that many feminists have repudiated the Beauvoir–Firestone repression of embodiment, and so on. The question is not whether these are extreme voices but whether, in perhaps extreme form, they point to broader general forces at work in, and on, feminism. The forces to which I refer either constitute the body as an alien "other," a trap and prison for women, a biological victimization or, alternatively, trivialize the body, regarding it as not even something important enough to vehemently deny or put in its proper place. From Ti-Grace Atkinson's reduction of sexual identity to "genitals," no more important than "skin color, height and hair color,"[12] to Nancy Chodorow's declaration—in her rightly acclaimed and widely discussed book on parenting and gender—that human sexuality is largely, if not entirely a "social product" (though one might want to consider some limited "biological variables"[13]), our embodiment remains for feminists, as it was for Mill, a predicament and stumbling block.

If one turns to political sloganeering and feminism's language of description, ultra-liberal tenets stand out. Women are enjoined to *seize control* of their bodies, or be declared their owners. The body becomes property the woman can alienate, or not, as she freely chooses. Women are declared the sovereigns of their bodies. Although some cavil at the possessive tone of such calls, the deeper imperative—that freedom, now cast as "reproductive freedom," requires perfect, or nearly so, control over a dangerously unreliable body—goes unchallenged. Making the case for publicly funded support of pregnant women, for example, a Marxist feminist describes their condition as "pregnancy disability," terms that evoke images of injury, female incapacity, even invalidism.[14] My intent here is *not* to challenge "reproductive freedom," nor to debate abortion-on-demand, but to show how deeply suffused feminist discourse is with the prevailing paradigm.

The most salient point for now is this: liberalism's denial of our essential embodiment, a denial that is fundamental and imbedded in the ontological and epistemological bedrock of liberalism, not only bears specific, derisory outcomes for women, but threatens to implode the liberal self from within. Severed from our embodiment, we are in danger of losing the locus of our feelings and desires. Foucault argues that the rational, choosing self may comply willingly with the requirements of social discipline and order, but the suppressed bodily half pushes in another direction, toward emergence as therapy and confession. Neither of these bifurcated selves is free from social control. Indeed, if Foucault is correct, the bifurcated modern self, liberal and feminist, is *more* susceptible to manipulation, being inherently unstable. Too much is denied; too much is stripped away.[15] A genuine alternative to liberalism's discourse on the body must begin with a deep affirmation of our essential embodiment, and then build on that notion a vision of a situated self whose being takes form over time, in a concrete social place.

Recent Marxist-feminist discussions of "reproductive freedom" within a class society do not offer a genuine conceptual alternative. That is, endorsing an atomistic construal for purposes of making the case for control of the body and then affixing this construal to a socialist doctrine of "class" and to calls for male–female solidarity, is deeply inconsistent. The ontology of atomism erodes solidarity at its roots; moreover, one cannot coherently pose men, on the one hand, as an antagonistic sex-class with each individual man and woman thereby engaged in a sex-class conflict, or war, in which the woman's "reproductive freedom" is both a right and a weapon, and then go on to embrace a robust version of the new collective in which all previously oppressed men and women join hands to make the new world. From what? Class *wars* are not a sure and secure basis for later social harmony and cooperation. Marxist feminism's indebtedness to liberal formulations is clear in such accounts. By severing women's embodiment from its traditional symbolic link to images of the giving and sustaining of vulnerable human life, such theorists make less likely the possibility that this partial contribution of women might come to stand for the regenesis of society as a whole.[16]

Formulations for sex equality that push a demand for homogeneity, for a "de-gendering" of human identity and social relations, also reflect the atomistic *episteme*. The denial of the body, hence of difference becomes a prerequisite for sex equality. Let me explain. One central characteristic of liberalism, remember, is a stripping away of distinctive features of personal identity and social location as one takes on an abstract, public identity and enters the liberal public sphere. Obligations and choices in that sphere derive from the rationally conceived interests of such stripped down individuals. Important feminist arguments for sex equality involve the extension of this process *into* the private sphere. The self is to be thinned-out even further as one's embodied distinctiveness is no longer seen as essential to one's identity.

If one examines the view of human nature, the human subject, and the individual featured in the background or foreground of arguments that require homogeneity as the basis for equality, it doesn't take long to recognize a rather shapeless figure, familiar to all students of Western liberal thought, lurking in the shadows. I refer to the human being conceived as a blank slate, *tabula rasa*, who starts off life *sans* "givens," or any stubborn "nature" of his or her own. Like so much plastic putty, *tabula rasa* is molded by external forces, or what B. F. Skinner would call the "contingencies of reinforcement." Thus we become infinitely easy to indoctrinate or to change—in theory. That this, too, denies the body is evident in calls for "androgyny" as a prerequisite for or, indeed, as the definition of equality between the sexes.

In visions of androgyny human bodies disappear. The term has been dusted off, stripped of its deeply sexed roots and previous mythic meaning, and redefined as completely flexible and interchangeable "roles" for men and women; as the elimination of all gender "asymmetry" and, for good measure, as the fusion of all "positive" traits, the elimination of everything that is presently weak or "undesirable" about either men or women as presently constituted. Our sexed, embodied identities are declared limiting and we are enjoined to achieve a higher identity by "transcending" sexual gender. The full achievement of an androgynous world is possible, then, only with the total elimination of sex roles and the "disappearance...of any biological need for sex to be associated with procreation." At that fateful moment, "there would be no reason why such a society could not transcend sexual gender."[17] The achievement of this fully androgynous person and society requires major social surgery—the radical completion of liberalism's historic trajectory to constitute a "weightless" self.

Equating difference with domination, embodiment with oppression, the only way out is to eliminate difference, to repress embodiment. By defining "asymmetry" as sex inequality, male dominance, and female oppression, androgynist feminists deepen a view of social reality that downgrades women's contributions and magnifies those of men. Rather than challenging the terms of male dominant society on the basis of its respective valuation of men and womens' worlds, and its negative construal of difference, differences themselves are attacked as the foundational root of sexual injustice. By conflating differences with domination, such feminists have little choice but to embrace a picture of a social world in which sexual differences are blurred or are no longer interesting and in which human beings have become so flexible that "roles" can be interchanged at will.[18]

To summarize, briefly: the feminist formulations I have criticized, abstracting from our essential embodiment, conjure up a world of identical, or nearly so, social atoms, thus extending ultra-liberalism's atomistic image of the subject into all spheres of life. These social atoms are enjoined to behave in a manner consonant with self-interest for if they recognized their "true" self-interests both individual freedom and social good would result. Traditional notions of identity, social relations, and authority are dismissed; tensions between human beings and their society evaporate (in the ideal world); and, ultimately, gender disappears as a criterion of status and "individuals are characterized in terms of ageless, androgynous personhood."[19] This is not at odds with our era—it is in harmony with it. In the long run it is self-defeating, for it cannot account for central aspects of our embodied existence and our social experience. In other words, this vision creates a self that cannot be sustained—that is so "weightless" it would evaporate were it not for the fact that, since it has become dogma, the way liberal society celebrates and explains itself, those previously excluded from this liberal definition are constrained to make their dissent precisely through its terms.

THE FAMILY AS THE ROOT OF OPPRESSION

That feminism's image of family relations, values, obligations, and purposes presumes a prior, if unacknowledged, embrace of atomism is evident not only in much of the early condemnatory treatment of families but in less obvious ways: in the reduction of the family to functionalist and instrumental terms; in formulations that empty families of deeper meaning *to* individual subjects and *for* social life; and in more recent defenses of family life that celebrate the notion of "nonbinding" as the basis for a new family. I have traced these treatments of the family in detail and I will not repeat myself here.[20] To clarify: I am not denying that families can be, and sometimes have been, coercive and damaging and that, historically, women have been submerged within family life in a way that men have not. But the patriarchal family is a vulnerable, weak institution. Capitalism and the atomism I have already described have eroded patriarchy's historic base. Men take their place in the social world *qua* men, not *qua* fathers, and there is no evidence that male authority in any of its public, institutionalized forms is dependent upon paternity. We certainly have male dominance of institutionalized forms of legitimate power but this is not necessarily patriarchy. One might compellingly argue that to describe modern familial relations as patriarchal distorts, but to what end? That end may be to extend liberal contractarianism into the arena of personal and intimate relations. To the extent that we view persons as owners of themselves rather than essentially part of a wider social surround, all human ties are put under pressure to redefine themselves in line with atomistic construals.

It is not my task to evaluate the justice in these feminist analyses and demands but to locate them in a discursive web. If one looks at choices of descriptive language together with terms of ideal evocations—all point to the conclusion that feminism's theory of the family, whether to damn it or to rescue it, purified of the taint of traditional authority and sexist history, makes sense *only* as part and parcel of ultra-liberal discourse. The woman is viewed as a preposited sovereign self whose selfhood has been denied under terms of male domination; her freedom, therefore, requires dissolving the locus of that domination. As I stated, the family does not fare well within this frame—one that views persons as proprietors of themselves. Michael J. Sandel sums up the dilemma in which liberals place themselves:

> But we cannot regard ourselves as independent in this way without great cost to those loyalties and convictions whose moral force consists partly in the fact that living by them is inseparable from understanding ourselves as the particular persons we are—as members of this family or community or nation or people, as bearers of this history, as sons and daughters of that revolution, as citizens of this republic. Allegiances such as these are more than values I happen to have or I "espouse at any given time." They go beyond the obligations I voluntarily incur and the "natural duties" I owe to human beings as such. They allow that to some I owe more than justice requires or even permits, not by reason of agreements I have made but instead in virtue of the more or less enduring attachments and commitments which taken together partly define the person I am.[21]

One possible alternative to the way in which familial ties and obligations get construed as oppressive and unduly constraining, within the terms of the atomist-contract model, is offered by an image of a *social compact*. The social compact puts pressure on ultra-liberalism and narrow contractualism without sliding into a celebration of the past or of total community. I shall explore briefly the way in which the contractarian and compact images structure different evaluations, not

only of the family but of women and their historic identities.
One of the ironic dimensions of ultra-liberal critiques of the
family is the unflattering and disparaging evaluation of women's
historic lives and practices it secretes.

Within the social compact, women's historic identities as
wives, mothers, and community beings are not sealed-off and
devalued using the atomist male as the standard of self. This
need not imply an uncritical embrace of prior ways of being
but it does mean one is less likely, from within the compact
frame, to go all the way with those who find in the past only
so much detritus to junk. Within the contract image, remember,
women's identities, inseparable as they are from families and
the human life cycle, are necessarily delegitimated: they do
not get writ large on the social screen as emblematic of a society
committed to the protection of the vulnerable, to an ethic of
care and responsibility. But inside the compact ideal, these
contributions signify society as a caring place, one protective
of specific ties, sustained by a sense of history and collective
memory, valuing diverse ways of being, promoting a working
reconciliation with nature.[22]

Thus the compact image puts immediate pressure on instrumental and technological politics, on narrow rationalism, and
on human domination of other life forms. More fully amplified,
the ethos I here suggest could serve as *one* basis for democratic
renewal, for a social world that taps our human capacity for
participatory responsibility and moral freedom free from the
arrogant presumption that what we require is greater control,
and an enhanced capacity to manipulate the human and natural world. For the liberal vision is deeply flawed as an account
of our political and moral life and experience. In Michael Sandel's words, "within its own terms,...stripped of all possible
constitutive attachments, [we are] less liberated than disem-
powered." The "sovereign subject," he concludes, "is left at sea."[23]

Not marking this "moral frailty" and the thin, rigid society
atomized contractarianism serves to constitute, feminists, too,
are threatened by the derailment of the liberal project. This
project is even now unraveling in our era—as extreme reactions
in the form of cults, robust evangelicalism, and so on indicate—
for the atomist air cannot sustain, over time, shared human

life; it cannot constitute, over time, robust human identity. Liberalism, finally, fails to redeem its own most cherished and liberating promises. This suggests a reconsideration of the ties that have linked women, symbolically, morally, socially, to worlds of family and community rather than seeing only the oppressive aspects and embracing instead male-created and sustained values of liberal market society including its instrumentalism and contractarianism.

Let me suggest some alternatives that both highlight ultraliberalism and point to a possible way out, if feminism is to become more reflective about its enterprise. One key question is our relation to history and tradition: can we, if we will it, repudiate history or reconstrue it to suit our current sensibilities? Or might a rethinking of history and tradition offer us, if we have eyes to see, the living embodiment of vital conflicts. In *After Virtue*, Alasdair MacIntyre quotes the philosopher John Anderson as urging us "not to ask of a social institution, 'What end or purpose does this serve?' but rather 'Of what conflicts is it the scene?' "[24] The family, and our relation to it, is the scene of conflicts that go to the heart of what we mean when we speak of human beings and their social worlds.

For family images tie us to that moral particularity which is an essential and necessary feature of our personal and social identities. We find our moral selves, our agency as persons, in and through our membership, first, in families, then in wider social networks of friends, kin, co-workers, comrades, and finally up to and including citizenship in the polity. We do not begin as beings with duties to man as such or as citizens with abstract political obligations as such. Instead, in MacIntyre's words, "without those moral particularities to begin from there would never be anywhere to begin;...it is in moving forward from such particularity that the search for the tool, the universal consists. Yet particularity can never be simply left behind or obliterated. The notion of escaping from it into a realm of entirely universal maxims...is an illusion and an illusion with painful consequences. When men and women identify what are in fact their partial and particular causes too easily and too completely with the cause of some universal principle, they usually behave worse than they would otherwise do."[25]

As a family member one is a most particular being. In challenging the terms of male domination, the feminist perspective too readily—I criticize—slid past that moral particularity which is not only an essential aid to self-definition but an important barrier to premature leaps into abstract universalisms that invite arrogant pacts with the *Weltgeist*. Wholly voluntarist communities of like-minded adults cannot provide a substitute for this basic moral grounding—cannot offer an alternative for the intergenerational roots of moral identity. As vital and nurturing as such communities may be, they tend toward a mimesis of liberal society in their age, sex, and class homogeneity and their delimited, functional ends; hence, they cannot serve as the symbolic base for the regenesis (as I have called it) of the human community. The ties do not go deep enough; they do not extend far enough into the past; they do not reach out far enough into the future. Where are old and dying people? Ill and infirm? Grandparents? Unborn? Newborn?

As Stanley Hauerwas points out, if we are to learn to care for others we must first learn to care for those to whom we find ourselves joined by accident of birth.[26] These commitments, in turn, are essential to our public life—if that life is to be grounded in an image of compact rather than contract. For, to "imagine a person incapable of constitutive attachments such as these is not to conceive an ideally free and rational agent, but to imagine a person wholly without character, without moral depth."[27] Our brief example of this factor is the connection drawn by Carol McMillen between our particular and our public selves: "It is only because there are relations between people which are exclusive and particular in character—those between husbands and wives, between siblings, between parents and children, between friends—that we are able to make the judgments we do about the plight of orphaned children."[28] This is just a beginning, to be sure, but without *this* beginning, for which there is no substitute, our lives would be infinitely more impoverished than they are by the atomism and litigiousness of contemporary life. We are born with a past. To see that simply as a deformation is to deform the present. Thus far feminists, beyond evocations of a wholly abstract future community of completely free persons whose constraints are voluntaristically and rationally chosen, have not tackled these vital matters.

My hunch is that there is more going on, in the repudiation or reductionistic treatment of families, than the understandable fear that any evocation of some characteristic "good" or "excellence" in families, and in mothering, may lock women into predetermined social roles. The antipathy toward our familial selves and women's traditional identity lies deep in the roots of Western liberal discourse and is best described as the rationalist prejudice that opposes reason and passion, the public world of men to the private world of women, seeing the former as rational, the sphere of human agency, and the latter as the unthought realm of female emotion. Women, the "expressive beings" in this rationalist construal, should they want to get in on the world of "reason" and agency, must adopt the presumption that traditionally masculine activities alone exemplify both reason and agency. But this perpetuates the very soil in which existing presumptions take root. The fact that any talk of "maternal thinking"—despite current evidence of the gender gap—touches a raw nerve indicates the depth of our absorption in received notions of what is to count as action, what is the nature of reason. If one repudiates the tendency of many feminists to embrace the devaluation of the realm of "necessity" in favor of some sphere of pure "freedom," one leaves oneself open to the charge of longing for a return of the old female verities. In fact, what is involved is the creation of an alternative to the hold of atomism on our thought and practice, and the charting of forms of life that might nurture civic virtue as well as protect individual moral agency and freedom.

CITIZENSHIP: FROM SELF-INTEREST TO A CIVIC CULTURE

The destruction of traditional forms of authority and of political entities beneath the level of the state, the triumph of technocratic thinking, the entrenchment of unaccountable bureaucracies, the increased reliance on litigation and unpopular strategies through the courts to attain political ends, the displacement of a politics of commonalities in favor of a politics of what Sheldon Wolin calls "groupies"—all are hallmarks of the era. The weakening of intermediary institutions leaves the atomist self facing a powerful state. That state, in principle, is chastened by liberal and constitutional constraints. But the modern turn to social planners and engineers, and unelected elites to promulgate and execute public policy erodes restraints on state power. Moreover, the instrumental state does not speak to our longing as citizens to share some higher purpose and work toward some collective end. We desire to enlarge our identities as well as attain our interests. Liberal statism cannot satisfy these yearnings for deep citizenship; indeed, more democratic options and alternatives are often derailed, not fitting the self-interested mode.

In another essay, I sketched the terms of feminism's absorption in liberal statist philosophy and politics.[29] Feminism's reliance on the state is historically understandable and it is no simple indictment of mainstream feminists, or those radical and Marxist feminists who also rely on state power (particularly in the area of "reproductive freedom," legal freedom, policing to promote sex equality, etc.) to point this out. However, I aim to question the kind of dependency on the state this trails in its wake and the potential undemocratic trajectory of such dependencies. For example: in calling, simply, for takeover of child-rearing in whole or in part by public institutions, feminists may promote the extension of instrumental relations to additional spheres by transforming all persons as completely as possible into "institutionalized" beings, and deepening the rationalization of all aspects of contemporary life. This is the "disempowering" of the self cited by Sandel in the passage quoted above. (Clearly, I am not arguing against child-care but challenging functionalist approaches to this important matter.)

One dramatic way in which mainstream feminism—and, it should be noted, in a move opposed by antimilitarist feminists—capitulates to statism is in the so-called right to fight argument. In a brief against the all-male military draft, the National Organization for Women countered the constitutionality of such a draft in such a way that capitulation, not challenge, resulted. For NOW accepted the claim that compulsory universal military service is essential to the concept of citizenship in a democracy. In fact, the notion of citizenship originates not with the theory and practice of democracy but with Machiavelli. It was Machiavelli who first argued that popular participation in the creation of a revitalized polity is lodged in a collective will that finds its external embodiment in the armed (male) popular state. This militarization of citizenship is morally subversive of alternative notions and theories of citizenship.

The point here is *not* to debate the all-male draft. But it is, once again, to show how a repudiation of what NOW called "archaic notions of women's role in society" may propel feminists into the arms of legalist individualism and the image of a collective will embodied in the state. An alternative might involve the appropriation by feminist political theory of a civic identity that does not sever its ties with the richness of particular moral existence, nor deny its roots in a past that might instruct us, but at the same time does not simply "chain" us to tradition in some oppressive sense. It we step outside the ultra-liberal picture, we find important theoretical sources and moral teachers—Aristotle and Jane Addams among others, and I shall turn to both below. For missing from feminist theory, and sorely needed, is a vision of politics as the deliberate effort by human beings to order and direct their collective affairs and activities, and an ideal of the citizen as one who, in common with others, establishes ends for his or her society and evaluates these ends. What is fundamental about politics in this scheme is participation-action in, with, and against a social world as one constitutive feature of the broader community and one essential of the person.

The rigidities of atomism cannot capture this wider and deeper ideal of citizenship, in part because within the ultra-liberal frame neither human agency nor shared social purposes can be understood unless they are first pared down to the terms of self-interest. Citizenship is either bleached out altogether or incorporated in an impoverished way as just another resource to be "maximized." Here I think, despite Aristotle's well-known views on women's incomplete nature which I and others have trounced at length, feminists should make their own Aristotelian turn. One looks to Aristotle not for his bad teleology of female nature but for a vision of politics which remains living and robust. This is where he might instruct feminist thinkers—to develop an ideal of citizenship that challenges the narrow terms of formal-legalism without opting for overinflated images of some future public being, as one who has given his or her complete, unambivalent consent and total commitment to the new order.

In the Aristotelian account, the human being as *actus humanus* discovers his or her own potentiality, reveals himself or herself to others, within a frame that links individual actions with moral responsibilty for a wider human network without submerging the individual into a social "mass" in the process. This brings me to Jane Addams, a figure I believe feminists should reconsider sympathetically. She shared civic humanism's high estimation of political activity, as Susan Tennenbaum points out in a recent essay.[30] But rather than disparaging women's traditional identities she saw them as one—*not the only*, but *one* possible basis or grounding for political being and identity, one *entree* into citizenship. Her civic humanism was no austere self-abnegation in behalf of the common good; instead, she invoked less austere feelings of mutual affection, compassion, and concern.

Addams called for nothing less than a new definition of the political—a plenary jolt to received meanings—shifting the symbolic foundation for the polity away from images of armed civic virtue to those of renewal and rebirth. It is with her challenge to the thin identity and impoverished meaning of ultra-liberalism that I shall conclude. Addams would be able to explain the current "gender gap" and she would have some advice on what to make of it. There is more to be said but if I have at least blurred or scrambled the ultra-liberal picture that holds us all captive, this essay has accomplished its purpose. Hannah Arendt captures what I am attempting here, by way of symbolic and theoretical challenge, when she links the image of natality or birth to that of political hope. She writes:

The miracle that saves the world, the realm of human affairs, from its normal, "natural" ruin is ultimately the fact of natality, in which the faculty of action is ontologically rooted. It is, in other words, the birth of new men [that is, human beings] and the new beginning, the action they are capable of by being born. Only the full experience of this capacity can bestow upon human affairs faith and hope, those two essential characteristics of human existence . . . that found perhaps their most glorious and most succinct expression in the new words with which the Gospels announced their "glad tidings": "A child has been born unto us."[31]

Ultra-liberalism cannot provide for a full exploration of the richness and importance of Arendt's evocative suggestions of the link between political hope and natality. I can only call for such an exploration. Women's identities and purposes, public and private, would look very different within a picture framed from Arendt's insight.

To conclude: to insist on a constitutive connection, yet a distinction, between citizen and private person is not to reinstate the gulf—the distance that ultra-liberalism requires. It is, instead, to insist that we forge that connection in a way that keeps steadily before our eyes the interlocked features of, but inescapable tension between, private and public hopes, values, identities and aspirations—a tension that is at once frustrating and enlivening. By seeking to eliminate this tension, by aiming for a world in which all good ends exist in complete harmony with one another, feminist atomism perpetuates a liberal project increasingly undermined by its own historic "successes." The "politics of limits" my alternative requires is not a frightened and distancing liberalism but a mordant realism, acquainted with human tragedy, sometimes awed by human triumph, always aware of the unavoidable pathos of living a human life. The subject of this politics is very different from ultra-liberalism's "thin" self, for he or she recognizes his or her "encumbrance" with a history and affirms a particular, thickly constituted identity with its loyalties and obligations as vital alongside manifestoes of freedoms. Recognition of limits becomes, paradoxically perhaps but powerfully, the touchstone of his or her humanity and the surest guarantee of freedom and civic virtue alike.

NOTES

1. The term is drawn from an essay by Charles Taylor, "Atomism," in *Power Possessions and Freedom: Essays in Honor of C. B. Mac-*

Pherson, ed. Alkis Kontos (Toronto: University of Toronto Press, 1979), pp. 39–61.

2. *Episteme* is a concept from Foucaultian discourse referring to "the total set of relations that unite, at a given period, the discursive practices that give rise to epistemological figures, sciences, and possibly formalized systems." (Michel Foucault, *The Archeology of Knowledge*, trans. Alan Sheridan [New York: Harper Colophon, 1972, p. 119.])

3. Taylor, "Atomism," p. 39.

4. Ibid., p. 41.

5. Ibid., p. 48.

6. Ibid.

7. See the discussion in Jean Bethke Elshtain, *Public Man, Private Woman: Women in Social and Political Thought* (Princeton, N.J.: Princeton University Press, 1981).

8. John Stuart Mill, *The Subjection of Women* (Greenwich, Conn.: Fawcett, 1970), p. 18.

9. Ibid.

10. Ibid., p. 141.

11. See my discussion in "Existentialism and Repressive Feminism," *Liberalism and the Modern Polity*, ed. Michael J. Gargas McGrath (New York: Marcel Dekker, 1978), pp. 33–62.

12. From Ti-Grace Atkinson, "Theories of Radical Feminism," *Notes from the Second Year: Women's Liberation*, ed. Shulamith Firestone (N.p., 1970), p. 33.

13. Nancy Chodorow, "On the Reproduction of Mothering: A Methodological Debate," *Signs: Journal of Women in Culture and Society* 6, no. 3 (1981), pp. 482–505.

14. Zillah R. Eisenstein, *The Radical Future of Liberal Feminism* (New York: Longmans, 1981). The term appears in the final chapter "The Capitalist Patriarchal State and Liberal Feminism."

15. Unpublished manuscript, William Connolly, "The Politics of Disciplinary Control."

16. Rosalind Pollack Petchesky, "Reproductive Freedom: Beyond 'A Woman's Right to Choose,'" *Signs: Journal of Women in Culture and Society* 5, no. 4 (Summer 1980), pp. 661–85, illustrates this claim. Powerful counter-evidence from anthropology which suggests that the actual and symbolic importance and vitality of female-linked activities, tied to images of rebirth, may ground cultures that feature a rough parity of power and authority between men and women may be found in Peggy Reeves Sanday, *Male Power and Female Dominance* (Cambridge: Cambridge University Press, 1981).

17. Ann Ferguson, "Androgyny as an Ideal for Human Develop-

ment," in Mary Vetterling-Braggin, Frederick A. Elliston, and Jane English, *Feminism and Philosophy* (Totowa, N.J.: Littlefield, Adam, 1977), pp. 62–63, 65.

18. See, for example, Nancy Chodorow, *The Reproduction of Mothering* (Berkeley: University of California Press, 1978), p. 219, where she points to resistance to radical alteration of "women's maternal function" as failure to see that this would serve women's *interest*.

19. Zelda Bronstein, "Psychoanalysis Without the Father," *Humanities in Society* 3, no. 2 (Spring 1980), p. 208.

20. Among my essays that touch on these themes are "Family Reconstruction," *Commonweal* (1 August 1980), pp. 430–31; and "Feminism, Family and Community," *Dissent* (Fall 1982), pp. 442–50.

21. Michael J. Sandel, *Liberalism and the Limits of Justice* (Cambridge: Cambridge University Press, 1982), p. 179.

22. What is being proposed here is *not* some nostalgic evocation of a past perfect time but a vision that can contain ways of being, past and present, that may help to break the hold of destructive forms of atomism on our thinking—even as individualities are protected.

23. Sandel, *Liberalism and the Limits of Justice*, p. 178.

24. Alasdair MacIntyre, *After Virtue* (Notre Dame: Notre Dame University Press, 1981), p. 153.

25. Ibid., pp. 205–6.

26. Stanley Hauerwas, "The Moral Value of the Family," in his collection of essays, *A Community of Character* (Notre Dame: Notre Dame University Press, 1981), pp. 155–66. See also Philip Abbott's *The Family on Trial* (University Park: Pennsylvania State University Press, 1981).

27. Sandel, *Liberalism and the Limits of Justice*, p. 179.

28. Carol McMillen, *Women, Reason and Nature* (Princeton, N.J.: Princeton University Press, 1982), p. 91. See also Jean Bethke Elshtain, "Antigone's Daughters," *Democracy* (April 1982), pp. 46–59.

29. Elshtain, "Antigone's Daughters."

30. Susan Tennenbaum, "Women Through the Prism of Political Thought," *Polity* XV, no. 1 (Fall 1982), pp. 90–102.

31. Hannah Arendt, *The Human Condition* (Chicago: University of Chicago Press, 1978), p. 247.

Robert Booth Fowler

V

Religion and Liberalism in the United States

I.

Religion and liberalism have existed together in American culture for a long time, sometimes waxing, sometimes waning, but the nature of their strange symbiosis has never been clear. In these days when, as always, both American liberalism and American religion are "in crisis" and yet in some versions flourish as never before, one may wonder how liberalism and religion intersect in our culture. However, while the connections between religion and American liberalism are a fascinating arena for rumination, they are notoriously hard to pin down. Some of the tethers which seem to bind them together have received intensive, if not necessarily satisfactory, study. Most, however, remain merely fields for speculation or assertion leaving one very much at sea, confident only that there must be connections in a liberal nation where religion has mattered so much. Meanwhile the evidence is scanty and the way treacherous.

In this essay I will explore two common ways in which liberalism and religion are often said to be interwined. One emphasizes our history and proposes that religious values and experience in the United States played a significant part in formulating American liberalism. A second contends that religion today (as in the past) has contributed to the legitimating ideology of American liberalism and its political and social order. This is the civic piety or civil religion thesis. Both of these views stress that religion has served liberalism in our national context by melding into liberalism, partially transforming it in the process. Both ideas are interesting and far from completely implausible. Yet I will argue that they have fundamentally mistaken the relationship between liberalism and religion. Religion has indeed served liberalism in the United States but not because the two have amalgamated to a considerable degree. Indeed, just the opposite is the case. Religion has aided liberalism by being a *refuge* from liberalism. It has been—and remains—so important in the United States, I will argue, because it provided an escape from liberal values, a place of comfort where individualism, competition, this-worldly pragmatism, and relentless nationalism do not hold sway. In a liberal country, with liberal citizens, religion is a place where one can come home (as the "real" home is less and less) and *then* emerge refreshed for the battles of life in the liberal world.

II.

The traditional analysis of the relationship between religion and liberalism (indeed, of our culture as a whole) is a historical one. Implying that religion is not centrally connected with liberalism today, it contends that religion has shaped the contours of American liberalism in the past to a considerable, if often imprecise, degree. Thus, to study the interconnections of religion and liberalism is to voyage to the past. This wedge into our problem is not the exclusive territory of intellectual historians, however. It has been a favorite approach of American political thinkers, of religious historians, and of not a few social scientists. In few cases does it stem from those unaware of the sometime hostilities between American religion (in some incarnations) and the liberal order and its norms; but in general, partisans of this view see a history in which religion and liberalism have largely gone hand-in-hand and conflict has been low overall. This insight is, I think, the great strength of their analysis in its multitude of forms. Their explanation for this fact—that liberalism in the United States is partly or largely the creation of our dominant (Protestant) religion in our past—is, however, both hard to support and (much more important) problematic at its heart.

The search for the roots of American liberal values in our religious background takes many routes, not surprisingly. The most common path is a fondness for analyses which sweeps across American history, plucking out one or several dimensions of liberalism which religion allegedly helped fashion (to an always undetermined degree). Candidates for religiously influenced aspects of American liberalism are almost as numerous as their partisans. Among those most often proposed are (1) pluralism, (2) individualism, and (3) liberal moralism.

The contribution of American religious experience to our liberal pluralism receives[1] (and merits) the most consideration. However, we must be cautious about what is said. This is true not just because what is under discussion here should be limited to political pluralism—diversity in political opinion, multiple interest groups, and the practice of group bargaining—but also because this pluralism has its substantial limits as everyone now acknowledges. Certainly religious diversity and pluralism characterized religion in the colonies and has since. Sidney Mead in *The Lively Experiment* describes the churches in America as traditionally sectarian, confident of their light and doubtful of others, not at all the gospel of liberal niceness amidst vague diversity which sometimes obtains today. In no way was this more obvious than the struggle within the vast panorama that was Christianity in eighteenth- and nineteenth-century America. Protestants warred with fellow Protestants, Protestants attacked Roman Catholics, while both Protestants and Catholics waged war against new religions, such as the Mormons. And few were loving in the struggle. If this was pluralism, it was a pluralism forged by necessity, not by choice.

Pluralism or sectarianism undoubtedly remains amid remarkable religious diversity in the United States. The host of different religious folk meant in the beginning Congregationalists, Episcopalians, Roman Catholics, Baptists, Methodists; later we added the Lutherans (of many varieties), the Disciples of Christ, the results of numerous Baptist and Methodist schisms, the black denominations, the Jews, the Christian Scientists, the Mormons, and, well, the list knows no end.

But how did this affect our political liberalism? The common view is that religious diversity offered or underlined a pluralist liberal model for politics which seemed natural and beneficial. Perhaps it did, or perhaps, more accurately, it made tolerance and thus political and other aspects of pluralism a necessity for national survival. On the other hand, religious pluralism obtained a good deal of encouragement and support from the eighteenth-century Enlightenment liberalism embodied in the First Amendment and our political system. While it had its limits, as polygamous Mormans learned, liberal political ideas may well have had more to do with sustaining religious pluralism than the reverse. We do not know, and untangling the skein of what was surely an interactive process is perhaps impossible.

American individualism is a second feature of American liberlism which some scholars suggest religion may have encouraged, deriving their theoretical roots, of course, from Weber's study of capitalism, the individual, and Protestantism.[2] There is no doubt that Protestantism in the United States has been peculiarly individualistic in its (relative) focus on individual salvation, resistance to mediators between the individual and God, and common doctrine of the priesthood of all believers. Nor is there reason to doubt the legion of historians who contend that religious individualism played a part in encouraging our liberal individualism. The contrast with the experience in more Catholic cultures only underlines this conclusion. But, again, was religious individualism a cause or an effect of our liberal individualism? The case can be argued both ways. Even if it has been more a cause as Weber could argue, it is not clear what the degree of influence has been, whether for example, it was more important than the British Whig tradition or Enlightenment views supporting individualism.

Then there is the thesis that the liberalism in our politics derives from American religious moralism with its tendency to see issues in terms of absolute right and wrong and to insist that only politics devoted to the realization of right and the defeat of wrong is acceptable.[3] Obviously, our liberal politics has teemed with moralistic crusades from antislavery to Prohibition to prayers in the public schools to abortion (both sides). How much religious moralism—often much exaggerated in the first place—has fostered this characteristic of our liberalism, however, remains unknown. It is an interesting idea; there is, perhaps, some truth to it; but what more can be said?

This brief survey of schools of thought which interpret the bond in American life between liberalism and religion as a historical tie founded in religion's influence on liberalism has in my hands repeatedly implied that evidence is skimpy, damagingly so. This is, I think, undoubtedly true; but if extensive, conclusive data is required for any discussion of religion and liberalism in the United States, this approach and any approach (including mine) is in major trouble from the start. So the problem with this traditional approach is not so much the quantity of data, or the inevitably ambivalent meaning of the sometimes generous evidence there is. The problem really is that these models of influence do not always see (or even suspect) that the process had to be an interactive one. They ask too rarely whether their models can just as plausibly be turned on their heads and aspects of American religion be made the child of strains of liberalism—as they often can be. Sometimes, moreover, there is scant sense of the process as one which has taken place over a long time, and continues to prosper today. What we often encounter is a list of static traits somehow imported into liberalism from religion at some time or times. This explanation, in short, is ordinarily not dynamic.

A welcome improvement may be found in William G. McLoughlin's *Revivals, Awakenings, and Reform: An Essay on Religion and Social Change in America 1607–1977* (1978).[4] McLoughlin's creativity lies in his attempt to formulate a sophisticated theory of dynamic interrelationships between liberal norms and culture and developments in religion in the United States. He avoids offering a static list of characteristics which somehow migrated from religion into liberal politics and remained there forever.

McLoughlin's theory is that there have been five periods of

religious awakening in American history, 1610–1640, 1730–
1760, 1800–1830, 1890–1920, and 1960–1990(?). He makes the
rather breathtaking contention that they "have been the shaping power of American culture from its inception," as altera-
tions in our religious temperament and belief have led to basic
changes which have significantly determined American society.

McLoughlin is clearly most interested in and informed about
the first two revolutions which he explores. He may have his
strongest case in his detailed and rich considerations on the
interaction of religion and culture in the seventeenth and eighteenth centuries. He is convincing when he shows the impact
of the Great Awakening as it affected the liberal ideas of the
revolutionary age. He is convincing when he shows the kind
of influence of the second Great Awakening 1800–1830: the belief in America's chosenness; the development of civil religion;
commitment to perfectionism and individual reformation; the
democratic faith in the individual; the urge to reform mankind.

Yet even here, and notably in his brief considerations on late
religious transformations, McLoughlin is not entirely convincing. For example, when he turns to the current "transformation" 1960–1990(?)—not the easiest ground for anyone, let us
admit—McLoughlin is disappointing. This is frustrating since
it is here that we could benefit most from his insights. For him
our age demonstrates clear evidence of another crisis in religion
and in liberalism, which may be summed up as the failure of
liberalism, liberal religion, and liberal politics. For Mc-
Loughlin the first response was that of the 1950's: the alleged
rush to traditional religion, Billy Graham and the rest. Then
in the 1960's Americans shunted aside traditionalism in religion and in politics as the Death of God, *The Secular City*, the
cults, etc., swept religion at exactly the same time as the New
Left went on the attack politically. Finally, McLoughlin views
the 1970's as an age of drift with long-run solution likely to be
(he predicts and hopes) a new religion and a new polity which
will offer some form of Judeo-Christian democratic socialism.

He may be right, though I do not know anyone today who
could look at either the religious or the political scene and put
any money on his predictions. McLoughlin ignores the alternative that conservative religion and a more conservative pol-

itics are the future in liberal America. This is, after all, the
day of the evangelist in religion and Ronald Reagan in politics.
But perhaps this is not quite the point. Where McLouglin is
on the mark is in his recognition that the interchange of religion and liberalism in American must be seen as a dynamic
process. It is one which requires us to do more than search for
the religious roots of liberalism and then rest. Rather it urges
us to go on to ask what the influences of religion are now as well
as in the past in American liberalism.

III.

A second major contender in seeking to explicate the inter-
relationship between religion and liberalism in America is the
civic piety thesis. This approach is far more attractive than the
first. It does not concentrate on this or that liberal norm or value
set as somehow *the* contribution of religion in the United States.
Instead, it looks at religion and liberalism in a broader and
more dynamic relationship and asks how they have served each
other. For our purposes, the issue is how religion has served
liberalism in America, apart from its putative influence regarding specific liberal values. The answer which students of civic
piety give is in a metamorphosed form religion has legitimated
American liberalism—and its liberal political order.

The modern pioneer of the idea of a "civil religion" or civic
piety was Robert Bellah in a famous 1967 article in *Daedalus*.
Bellah has continued to be a fertile contributor to the ongoing
discussion about this idea. He contends that public life in the
United States operates under a religious framework which,
while not explicitly Christian, clearly employs many traditional Christian categories now transferred to a secular world,
a theme he has pursued in several books, such as *Beyond Belief*
and *The Broken Covenant*.[5] He notes, for example, that the
Puritan notion that America is special and that Americans
have a special mission in world history has often received political expression from presidents and other significant public
figures. As evidenced in Bellah's key source, major public documents, political leaders have commonly seen that mission as
derived quite specifically from God. For Bellah, Lincoln was

an especially poignant and sensitive exponent of the link of
God and the American destiny albeit in ways, as he said in his
Second Inaugural, we could not know. John F. Kennedy, a
hundred years later, was still offering the same public affir-
mations and by that action still giving life to civil religion, the
religion of God-blessed America.

Needless to say, Richard Nixon used civic piety, like much
else, for all it was worth during his presidency. He constantly
invoked God and affirmed his closeness to the American experience. He also declared our essential innocence as part of
God's blessing. That Nixon proclaimed these things easily made
for a study in contrast with Lincoln who thought God's relations
with the United States were complex and ultimately myste-
rious. Bellah thought that while this revealed a difference in
understanding which was a devastating commentary on Nixon,
the essential point remained. Both followed the tradition of
civil religion and both were believers. So has Ronald Reagan,
of course, and he too appears to be a believer.

The work that Bellah has done has finely delineated the civic
piety idea; but, as he would agree, he is by no means the only
one or the first to articulate the threads of the current consideration of civil religion. From within the history of religion
probably the most admired writer on this subject has been
Sidney Mead, especially in his work *The Lively Experiment*.
More than Bellah he tells the story of our national religion
with historical perspective. For Mead, the national religion
grew steadily over time and by the Civil War was unmistakably
established. After the Civil War till now there have really been
two religions in the United States, Christian denominations
and the American faith, the stepchild of American Christianity. It is Mead's view that the two forms of religion in America
have often been intertwined and mutually supportive. He does
not think our supposed separation of church and state has saved
the churches of the nation from dominance by the liberal culture and political order around them. Indeed, throughout much
of our history the churches "found themselves as completely
identified with nationalism and their country's political and
economic system as had ever been known to Christendom."[6]

Our national religion assumes, in Mead's version as in Bellah's, that somehow our nation is to be the agent of the divine. It urges Americans to be a community of people searching to discover and live God's ordained life together. Yet at the same time it respects the individual and intellectual and political pluralism. Mead emphasizes the democratic aspects of the American faith more than Bellah, meaning a faith in people and their self-government on earth rather than in the specific forms of our democratic system.

A recent example of the continuing use of the civic piety mode of analysis is Marshall Frady's remarkable study, *Billy Graham*, the best modern argument for the deep interweaving of the liberal state and Christianity in America.[7] Frady's *Billy Graham* is a product of the disillusioned 1970's, but it insists that the events of the 1960's and 1970's did not derail widespread faith in a God-blessed America, Graham leading the way. To be sure, Frady notes that Graham claims he rejects civil religion and strongly supports separation of church and state, but while Frady believes such claims were and are sincere, he does not think they are accurate.

According to Frady, Graham revealed his loyalty to civic piety or religion through his aggressive role as a servant and companion of presidents beginning with Eisenhower and not easing until after the embarrassing denouncement of his friend, Richard Nixon. This constituted a very public linkage of America and Christianity in a way that to Graham apparently presented no problems at all. Graham has also revealed his loyalties as he has reacted with fright toward any forces who appear to challenge the American social order, including Vietnam War protestors and Martin Luther King and others in the civil rights struggles of the 1960's. Vietnam is especially important. Graham supported the war without reservation until it was almost over and does not yet regret his stance. He still, Frady concludes, believes in continuing American innocence at home and abroad and does not hesitate to lend his name to sanctify it.

However, despite (or, perhaps, because of) the vogue this approach has enjoyed, it is not without its skeptics. The more gentle, such as Martin Marty,[8] note that the notion of a civic piety is a "loose construction" which can and does mean almost anything—or have almost any effects—depending on the hands employing it. What really is the "civil religion"? What is "civic piety"? Are they the same? Are they religions? Moreover, Marty contends, even when the notion receives a careful and lucid formulation it is almost inevitably too simplistic, stressing only one side of its supposed efforts (the conservative legitimating ones).

A harsher view, which Marty also sympathizes with, suggests the whole idea is a fantasy of overactive scholarly minds. John Wilson best speaks for this view in his *Public Religion in American Culture.*[9] He maintains that no one can find a civil religion in America. Rituals and dogmas are everywhere in politics but demonstrated coherent linkage to religion is absent. Moreover, what they signify so obviously changes over time, revealing not a set of timeless truths rooted in religion but a set of images involved in particular time and circumstance. Thus our political rituals and dogmas are a little like proverbial eels. Whenever one reaches out for them, they take a different form, direction, place. Worse, while an eel can somehow be located, civil religion cannot be. It is, Wilson suspects, an artifact of an uncertain age, an intellectual creation by those and for those who seek some port in the storm.

One wonders, though, if this is quite the end of the story. A formal civic religion or a less formal civic piety may not be easy to demonstrate—much less a case for religion fashioning and supporting it—but it is no fantasy. Experience as well as social science data suggests there are at least some legitimating aspects of religion and liberal America. I sat in a church of my denomination during the July 4, 1982, weekend in the midst of a poor section of sadly depressed Flint, Michigan, and listened to my usually somnolent coreligionists suddenly transform themselves as they eagerly sang "America the Beautiful." It was the sermon for the day and the symbolic significance of the suddenly raised voices in the church was clear. Such an experience merely mirrors what poll data establishes. Clergy and churchgoers of all religious persuasions report generally strong support for the American political order. It is no surprise, then, that no major religious denominations have attacked our political system in any basic way. In the pews and even at national headquarters of supposedly radical mainstream Protestant denominations there is no serious religious opposition to American liberalism. Yes, there are dissatisfactions with one or another policy and there are particular churches where dissent runs deeply. But they are curiosities which from an overall perspective are mere asterisks in the data.[10]

This does not necessarily mean that the support is intensely cultivated at church. "America the Beautiful" is not sung every Sunday and "The Star Spangled Banner" is rarely heard. It is a mistake to make most forms of religion or churches or clergy or laity into highly political entities bent on propping up the liberal state. This happens and certainly real opposition is rare but ordinarily the process operates differently if no less potently. Perhaps the most significant support for the liberal order, one should recognize, comes in organized religion's basic pursuit of other agendas than the political. What this means is that religion in America is not basically, or even often, concerned with sustaining liberalism much less contributing to a civic piety. From the world of politics, or at least the speeches of presidents, such "religion" may gain expression, but it is not a creation of religion in America, and certainly not the churches, nor is it in general a concern of theirs. Religious Americans like almost all citizens are sympathetic to our political order, but they are not especially directed to sustain it much less formulate or participate in a civic piety to sustain it.

Of course, for those who are involved in studying politics but have little contact with religion in America, religion can seem very political today. Catholic bishops make the news denouncing the nuclear arms race or abortion; the National Council of Churches speaks out on this and that; the Moral Majority demands school prayers, a strong defense policy, support for capitalism, banning pornography, and so much more; Jewish interest groups insist on ever more aid for Israel; and so it goes. Yet the reality in the pews, the sermons and homilies, and the denominations—despite a few pronouncements from the top— is so very different as students of religion know. There politics is rarely heard and rarely discussed. This is, again, not merely a matter of what the surveys show; it is a matter of what one experiences on Friday night, on Saturday, and, above all, on

Sunday morning. Even a casual listening to the T.V. evangelists, men often said to be highly political, confirms how very apolitical in any overt sense American religion normally is, and thus how little it is devoted to protecting the American liberal society, much less supporting a civic piety. Standing with a crowd on Palm Sunday 1982 in front of a large "socially conscious" church for the blessing of palms, I saw a poor drunk come up and curse the faithful as terrible hypocrites. He shouted that they did not care about him and his kind. A perceptible shock swept the gathered faithful—but for a few seconds only. A young man or two gave the drunk some money and he staggered off and the crowd turned to something much more important to it and soon shared the blessed palms. As quickly as it had come overt politics was far away again, blessedly far away, and the relief was obvious.

Even more problematic is the civic piety perspective as it relates to liberal *values* as opposed to (liberal) American culture. That there is some vague entity we might call a civic piety and that it does link the religion and the state is not implausible as long as one does not exaggerate the degree of political awareness and interest in American religious worlds. Yet this does not really get at what specifically is the dynamic *in terms of values* between American liberalism and Christian (for that is what we must necessarily talk about) religion. The more we ask the question, the more the civic piety view falls silent. It is not about values, basically, but about the legitimation of the state culture by the church. In this sense, it may tell us something about the United States, but very little about liberalism and religion. This, in the end, is its great drawback.

IV.

The case that is crying out to be made is quite a different one. I would argue, in fact, that much too much is made of linkages between religion and liberalism or the liberal order in the United States and suggest an alternative hypothesis. Religion in the United States is basically an *alternative* to the liberal order. Moreover, as an alternative, religon has had to choose serving either as a refuge from liberalism or as a challenge to liberalism. It has chosen to be a refuge and in this choice lies the basis for its real link to the liberal state and society, one more subtle and consequential than those ordinarily argued. I mean "refuge" in the religious sense of the word, retreat in this case as a place where one can escape liberalism, or its costs. This need not, and I shall argue it does not, imply that American religion and liberalism are not locked in a supportive relationship, but it is hardly one in which religion has been and is little more than a cheerleader for Americans as they live out their lives in liberal America. Quite the contrary.

There are two ways in particular in which religion serves as a refuge from American liberalism. It is a refuge from (1) liberal rational skepticism and (2) liberal individualism, our peculiar, relentless, and demanding moral ideal for the human person. The refuge from skepticism of course involves the fact that religion and the churches are about absolute truth, about a realm in which there are certainties, no matter how much they may evaporate when one thinks about them in terms of concrete morality or public policy (though for many of the religious they do not evaporate then). This point can hardly be overemphasized. It is no accident that "conservative churches are growing" for the well-documented reason that they provide the certainties which modern liberalism does not and which, perhaps, liberalism inevitably cannot offer. Similarly, the enduring strength of the Roman Catholic Church continues to turn on its institutional and doctrinal orthodoxies, despite Vatican II, guitar masses, and hip priests. On the other hand, surely it is equally unsurprising that mainline Protestant churches have failed to prosper in the age of skeptical liberalism. They provide rarer refuge from the imperatives of liberalism as we experience it. Indeed, they are its religious children.[11]

Skepticism, of course, in modern liberalism is firmly rooted in a certain rationalism which religion too, on the whole, rejects. Here one thinks of the empirical pragmatic, calculating rationalism so dominant in the practical reason of American liberalism. Unless one thinks of religious believers as exemplifications of Pascal, shrewdly taking religion as a wager in case there is another life—and there is no evidence they think this way—then religion is about something else. It is not, as we know, about reason, in fact, certainly not according to the extensive data we possess on the religious in our nation. It is about faith (for example 95 percent of Americans believe in God, 80 percent in Christ as God) for which there really is no empirical evidence. Even less is it about pragmatic calculation. Faith and the central Christian doctrine of grace—salvation by God's choice—are simply an entirely different approach to understanding and dealing with life.

Equally different, perhaps, is the aesthetic dimension which is so much a part of religion. Its forms may vary. The music, the poetry of the service, the ceremony of the liturgies, the architecture of the church, all vary from church to church, denomination to denomination. But that religion in America has an aesthetic dimension is certain. Yet where in pragmatic liberal rationality is such an appeal to the aesthetic? Maybe there are a few Benthams for whom the calculations of life fulfill this role, but, one suspects, not many.

Equally, religion offers a refuge from the American liberal's central ethic of the individual. In all the discussion of the "me decade" (which seems to be lasting far longer than a decade), or the broader concern with the individual which *is* liberalism today (however variously affirmed), or the celebration of the individual which is justly famous as the heart of the American political tradition, it is often forgotten that there are other worlds, especially worlds of practice, in the United States. Equally forgotten sometimes is how attractive these worlds are to many citizens. I do not mean the long-trumpeted groupiness of American life. That can be neatly incorporated within American liberalism and long has been. Pluralism is merely the liberal's social ideal, or at least approved reality. I do not even mean such mundane, but perhaps noteworthy, facts as our marriage rate which far exceeds our much touted divorce rate.

Religion, as our case at hand, goes well beyond these points in being a refuge from the self in at least two ways that are of great significance. It offers a refuge in its very affirmation of transcendence. It is sometimes hard for those who are not religious to understand just how important this fact can be to the believer. After all, belief in some kind of God(s) is integral to any ordinary definition of religion and certainly is so in American religion. Moreover, in Christianity this God is invariably portrayed as one who is with us—"lo I am with you always"—and as a Being who allegedly cares for every person no matter how desperate his or her life. Christianity also obviously tries to address the loneliness of death and potential nothingness, a realm where liberalism is utterly silent.

In this context one thinks of Freud's enlightenment liberal essay, *The Future of an Illusion*. For Freud, the liberal skeptic, religion was an appalling error. Yet he was well aware of how belief in transcendence functioned as a refuge, as a powerful consolation for people. It told them that there was an explanation for their suffering and there was a basis for hope. While he believed we could do without such a crutch and that we should as well, he acknowledged the pain of individual suffering which he felt was the root of religion. In this he was far more acute than many secular liberals today for whom religion in America is a fossil which, inexplicably, endures despite the gentle winds and rains of liberalism.

Perhaps more important in ordinary human terms is religion's role as a refuge from relentless individualism in its social, even communal, aspects on earth. Partly this is a matter of religion as the community of believers whether seen in international, national, denominational, or local church terms. Studies establish very clearly the appeal of the church in this sense for couples who begin creating their own would-be community when they enter childbearing and child-rearing ages. It is at this development stage that dissident, alienated, and disinterested young people often begin their trek to (or back again to) churches. Study after study documents the appeal for young families of the church as a community (or would-be community). They also establish the attractive power of particular churches which provide such satisfying social life. Clearly for many Christians and other religionists in America the church more or less approximates the community they seek but too rarely find in liberal society. One should note too that an extremely important reason for defections from religion, one that is much more prevalent than religious skepticism, is the failure of individual churches to be community-like. This can involve the emergence of factions, competition, or pettiness, in a church. It can involve a lack of friendliness and a sense of impersonality. Either way, churches guilty of these characteristics inevitably lose members and fail to garner many new ones. They are, in short, not refuges and they pay for this fact.[12]

Apart from the religious idea of the community of believers and the practical social needs and expectations which surround every church, there is another aspect of religion in America as a social refuge. This is the widespread belief in our culture that religion is *for* the social and *about* the social. That is, regardless of whether religions do promote bonding among people, the expectation that they should remains. The idea persists that religion is about love above all else, and not just love of God, and that religious people and their houses of worship should manifest this love. Theologians and clerics may debate, but studies of attitudes of people, especially toward churches, demonstrate how routinely people expect religion to be about community—as well as how often they are disappointed when they discover it is also very much about quite ordinary people in a liberal culture at best ambivalent about this goal, outside the family. The point is that the culture has anointed the church as well as the family as the "haven" from a liberal world and, for what they are worth, statistics today suggest that more may find something of that haven in the church than at home. But this is not merely a popular judgment. Such a view for example partly lies behind Daniel Bell's and some other neoconservatives' desire to see religion revive in the United States.[13]

As Marx was so well aware, community is a form of order, often a demanding one—he wanted not an individual with rights, but an individual social being, something else again. This is exactly what community means for many small religious groups from the Amish to some of the newer religions of the 1960's and 1970's, including the Hare Krishnas or the followers of Reverend Moon. It is the aspiration of Hasidic Jews and some fundamentalist Protestants. And it is at least a memory for many Catholics and other Protestants, a memory which in some churches is still quite alive.

In short, from several angles religion in America aspires (if not necessarily self-consciously) to be a refuge from individualism—and sometimes is.

V.

The larger question is, though, why are religion and the churches not more of a *challenge* to liberalism. We have seen already in Part III that the evidence in practice, the evidence from the pews, hardly suggests such a challenge. A refuge it may well be, but our evidence leads us to observe that it is a refuge which appears to dwell comfortably within a larger acceptance of the liberal order. Why are there not more challenges from out of the house of refuge? Why is refuge the path rather than challenge when religion and liberalism would seem to denote two rather different world views in the United States?

This query is reinforced when one thinks of the views of great minds of the twentieth-century European world arguably in the liberal tradition, such as Freud or Camus. I am struck by how often they were contemptuous of the value of religion for their liberalism and convinced that it should be dispensed with. Freud's belief was really that religious belief was a denial of civilized liberal individualism and Camus in his famous discussion with the priest in *The Plague* pointedly insisted that he wanted no God who let innocent children die. The same animus is not really present in the post-1945 American liberal thought. On the whole religion is simply absent from the work of theorists from Robert Dahl to John Rawls. The effect is the same, though: liberalism need not be tied to religion, indeed should not be. It is not accurate to say that here liberal theorists have ordinarily perceived religion to be a challenge to liberalism, but its fundamental incompatibility with liberalism is taken for granted. And obviously religious thinkers—activists such as Reinhold Niebuhr or Martin Luther King, Jr.—seem to have gained a great deal of their acceptance within the liberal pantheon despite their "puzzling" religiosity, rather than because of it.

Yet in our culture, religion and a vague liberalism go on hand in hand, despite intellectual thought and fashion with scant hint of incongruity (or challenge). Perhaps Marx was closer to the social truth than Freud or Rawls, perhaps religion and liberalism *are inseparable* and therefore religion can hardly pose a fundamental challenge to American liberalism. If Marx was correct, though, it is not because somehow churches and religion are part of a superstructure of thought in capitalist societies which elites self-consciously use to exercise hegemonic rule. This is a far too simple interpretation and one which strangely overlooks what we have seen: the sharp gaps that exist between key liberal ideas and central (Christian) religious ones. Something else is at work to explain the great strength of religion in the most powerful liberal society of human experience. May it not be that the differences between liberalism and Christianity suggest a good part of the answer? That is, is it not religion's very service as a refuge which explains its significant place in liberal America?

Religion does indeed commonly (though not necessarily) help American liberalism in practice. It does so by diffusing its costs, by being the refuge, rather than serving as a logical piece in liberal "hegemony." Aileen Kraditor's remarkable new book, *The Radical Persuasion*, contends that American Marxists at the turn of the last century misunderstood the complex needs and aspirations of the American working classes. She emphasizes how much they misunderstood the genuine importance of ethnic and religious ties and hung on to an unrealistic model of the worker as an economic person only. In this context, I would add that both critics and celebrants of liberalism in the contemporary United States underestimate the role religion plays—apparently needs to play—in many citizens' lives. It is important to them as a refuge and through this role it makes the liberal world they live in bearable and more attractive. As once with ethnic identification for immigrant workers, so today with religion for many, the results are the same. And the irony is that in a cultural sense Freud and Camus and Rawls were and are dead wrong. It is liberalism (in America anyway) which *needs* religion, needs it to provide an escape from itself. In practice it dares not do without religion, though its intellectual proponents and critics do not realize it.

The connectedness of liberalism and religion in the United

States, then, has a logic, even if it is not a logic commonly noted or mutually celebrated. It inevitably leads us on to a conclusion about liberalism in practice which theorists proclaimed in previous centuries whether by the voice of Edmund Burke or by that of Karl Marx. Somehow for a great many people liberalism is an *incomplete philosophy of practical life* and therefore will not succeed where it lacks a symbiotic (and supportive) relationship with worlds which can compensate for its incompleteness. In an old refrain, it does not provide for meaning, in terms of belief and in terms of social sharedness. Religion may not fill this need, though it appears to do so for many in the United States, but the need is there—and it is, despite Freud's "hopes," apparently an inexorable one.

Perhaps celebrants and practitioners of liberal thought should address its incompleteness and welcome religion as a possible ally. Perhaps eighteenth-century skepticism in modern dress is far less viable in human terms than it once seemed to the liberal "greats" and to their enlightenment intellectual descendants today. On a more practical level perhaps those concerned to preserve the liberal order in the United States should turn a far more sympathetic ear to religion and religious institutions. It is far less threatened by Jerry Falwell's admonitions on prayer in public schools, or Catholic campaigns regarding nuclear weapons, or the National Council of Churches' vague political leftism than it is by a decline in religion. For if our liberal order were shorn of the refuge from liberalism which religion provides, the consequences might be disastrous for liberalism in America. And yet, quite contrary to Marx, liberalism in America will not find in religion an eager or devoted ally or apologist. American religion, on the whole, is about other values than liberalism. Its relationship with liberalism will continue to be uneasy. If it continues to serve liberalism and our liberal order it will only be as unwitting ally, one which at its heart may, in fact, be an enemy, an enemy within.

For this reason those committed to our liberal order have an interest in the maintenance of the current boundaries of church and state in the United States. The current Supreme Court doctrine enunciated best in *Walz* v. *the Tax Commission* as

"benevolent neutrality" suggests proper balance. The idea is
that the state will smile on religion and churches as a group,
give them tax exemptions as Walz provided. But at the same
time it will not get close to religion. To be sure, the painful
thicket of alternative and sometimes competing religions is
part of the danger here, a big part perhaps. From a broader
perspective, however, perhaps more secular liberals should be
uneasy at granting too great a role to the alternate values
religions may propose as well as any decline of the church as
a refuge from liberalism. For religion in America, at its heart,
is not about liberalism and cannot be. It is liberalism's enemy
within, still largely quiet, but less and less so.

NOTES

1. Some useful literature: S. Mead, *The Lively Experiment* (New
York: Harper & Row, 1963); William Lee Miller, "American Religion
and American Political Attitudes," James Ward Smith and A. Leland
Jamison, *Religion in American Life* (Princeton, N.J.: Princeton Uni-
versity Press, 1961); William Clebesch, *From Sacred to Profane: The
Role of Religion in American History* (New York: Harper & Row, 1968),
chs. 3, 5, and 7; Walter Brownlow Posey, *Religious Strife on the South-
ern Frontier* (Baton Rouge: Louisiana State University, 1965); Edwin
Scott Gaustand, *Dissent in American Religion* (Chicago: University
of Chicago Press, 1973); H. Richard Niebuhr, *The Social Sources of
Denominationalism* (New York: Meridian, 1962); Andrew Greeley,
The Denominational Society (Glenview, Ill.: Scott, Foresman, 1972).
2. Max Weber, *The Protestant Ethic and the Spirit of Capitalism*
(New York: Scribner's, 1958); S. N. Eisenstadt, *The Protestant Ethic
and Modernization* (New York: Basic Books, 1968).
3. Citations in n.1 apply here; also see the helpful H. Richard
Niebuhr, "The Protestant Movement and Democracy in the United
States," James Ward Smith and A. Leland Jamison, *The Shaping of
American Religion* (Princeton, N.J.: Princeton University Press, 1966);
Sydney E. Ahlstrom, "The Puritan Ethic and the Spirit of American
Democracy," in George Hunt, ed., *Calvinism and the Political Order*
(Philadelphia: Westminister, 1965); Alan Heimert, *Religion and the
American Mind* (Cambridge: Harvard University Press, 1966); Sacvan
Bercovitch, *The Puritan Origins of the American Self* (New Haven:
Yale University Press, 1975); Larzer Ziff, *Puritanism in America* (New
York: Viking, 1973). Daniel Elazar dissents from the usual approach

from the perspective of regional variation in his interesting, "The American Cultural Mix," in *The Ecology of American Political Culture*, ed. Daniel J. Elazar and Joseph Zikmund (New York: Crowell, 1975).

4. William G. McLoughlin, *Revivals, Awakenings, and Reform: An Essay on Religion and Social Change in America: 1606–1973* (Chicago: University of Chicago Press, 1978).

5. Robert N. Bellah, "Civil Religion in America," in Russell E. Richey and Donald G. Jones, *American Civil Religion* (New York: Harpers, 1974); Robert N. Bellah, "American Civil Religion in the 1970's," in Richey and Jones; for a provocative discussion, also see Sandy Levinson, "The Constitution in American Civil Religion," *Supreme Court Review* (1979), pp. 123–51.

6. Mead, *Lively Experiment*, pp. 88, 157, chs. 5 and 8; idem, *The Nation with the Soul of a Church* (New York: Harper & Row, 1975).

7. Marshall Frady, *Billy Graham, A Parable of American Righteousness* (Boston: Little, Brown, 1979), pp. 240, 216, 214–15, 234–36, 232, 415–16, 412, 430, 418–19.

8. Martin Marty, "Two Kinds of Civil Religion," in Richey and Jones, p. 142.

9. John Wilson, *Public Religion in American Culture* (Philadelphia: Temple University Press, 1979).

10. George Gallup, Jr., and David Poling, *The Search for America's Faith* (Nashville: Abingdon, 1980); Thomas C. Campbell and Yoshio Fukuyama, *The Fragmented Layman: An Empirical Study of Lay Attitudes* (Philadelphia: Pilgrim Press, 1970); Kathleen A. Frankovic, *The Effect of Religion on Political Attitudes* (New Brunswick, N.J.: Rutgers University Press, 1974); Charles Y. Glock et al., *To Comfort and To Challenge* (Berkeley: University of California Press, 1967); Jeffrey Hadden, *The Gathering Storm in the Churches* (Garden City, N.Y.: Doubleday, 1969); Mary Hanna, *Catholics and American Politics* (Cambridge: Harvard University Press, 1979); Alfred Hero, Jr., *American Religious Groups View Foreign Policy: Trends in Rank and File Opinion, 1937–1969* (Durham, N.C.: Duke University Press, 1973); Lawrence Kersten, *The Lutheran Ethic: The Impact of Religion on Laymen and Clergy* (Detroit: Wayne State University Press, 1970); Harold Quinley, *The Prophetic Clergy: Social Activism Among Protestant Ministers* (New York: John Wiley, 1974).

11. Hadden, *Gathering Storm in the Churches*; Dean Kelley, *Why Conservative Churches Are Growing* (San Francisco: Harper, 1977); Hanna, *Catholics and American Politics*; Gallup and Poling, *America's Faith*.

12. Dean R. Hoge, *Converts, Dropouts, Returnees: A Study of Re-

ligious Change Among Catholics (New York: Pilgrim, 1981); John Kotre, *The View from the Border* (Chicago: Aldine, 1971).

13. For example, see Peter Clecak, *Crooked Paths: Reflections on Socialism, Conservatism, and the Welfare State* (New York: Harper, 1977); Peter Steinfels, *The Neo-Conservatives* (New York: Simon & Schuster, 1979); Daniel Bell, *The Cultural Contradictions of Capitalism* (New York: Basic Books, 1976).

Alan Stone

VI

Justifying Regulation

I.

In 1935, John Dewey wrote that the economic individualism of early liberalism was outmoded. Only through "organized social planning, put into effect for the creation of an order in which industry and finance are socially directed," could liberalism "realize its professed aims." To "regiment things and free people" was to be the goal of the new liberalism.[1] Indeed, the subsequent liberal agenda has focused upon programs designed to implement Dewey's dictum.

Yet the antigovernment ideas of Adam Smith and Herbert Spencer continue to capture the liberal imagination. They enjoyed a twentieth-century resurgence in the writings of Friedrich von Hayek and Ludwig von Mises. A new version of the "old" liberalism can be traced to the 1958 founding, at the University of Chicago, of the *Journal of Law and Economics*.[2] The journal from its inception has advanced, in a large number of very high quality articles, several themes. First, it has sought to show that the costs of government intervention usually outweigh the benefits. Second, it has advanced the thesis that the free market is a far more efficient and equitable institution than its critics have urged. Indeed, market mechanisms can readily be adapted to meet virtually any new economic or social problem. For example, tradable property rights can be created for the right to pollute or the right to broadcast, just as previous generations created tradable property rights in stock certificates. Third, the journal developed the complementary historical arguments that the era of free competition did not lead to the evils that many social critics charged and that regulation was more often than not instituted at the behest of business interests to attain stability and protect themselves from the hazards of competition. For example, one found in the early issues articles arguing that: (1) the charges of predatory conduct leveled at the old Standard Oil Company were untrue and (2) restrictive occupational licensure was instituted by professions seeking to restrict entry, and thereby charge monopoly rents for their services.[3] Interestingly, historians identified with the left also joined the chorus, claiming that regulation during both the Progressive Era and the New Deal was far more attributable to firms seeking cartel protection than to workers, consumers, or other groups seeking to redress grievances.[4]

This brief look at the modest beginnings of what has become part of the conventional wisdom already points to some of the sources of its appeal. First, what I will term the law-and-economics tradition does not nakedly apologize for the actions of big business. Witness, for example, the condemnation from that quarter of the Chrysler bail out. Condemnation is reserved, however, only for those instances in which businessmen seek government intervention. The law-and-economics ideology almost unreservedly applauds the actions of businessmen when undertaken in a market free of government interference. In general, it has advanced a theme that can be translated into a simple message that all can understand—competition is good, regulation is bad.

The second source of appeal that can be traced to its origins is one that has found favor primarily with intellectuals and opinion leaders whose ideas are transmitted to the public through the media. The appeal is very simply that the law-and-economics tradition provides a unified critical framework to interpret past events, challenge current policies, and prescribe imaginative alternatives. It is probable that this aspect of the law-and-economics tradition accounts for its magnetic appeal for so many first-rate scholars. The work of economist R. H. Coase, especially, provided the intellectual framework for so much subsequent effort designed to show the benefits of the free market and the harm imposed by regulation. In two remarkable pieces published in the second and third issues of the *Journal of Law and Economics*, Coase: (1) imaginatively applied property, contract, and market notions to radio and television spectra in place of FCC regulation, opening the way for the application of market mechanisms to other social phenomena and (2) reconceptualized the idea of social cost in such a way that one is compelled to assess the relative costs and benefits of different social arrangements, including government intervention. This notion led subsequent researchers in the law-and-economics tradition to argue in case after case that the net costs stemming from government regulation exceed those stemming from free market arrangements.

But if Coase brilliantly provided the underlying intellectual framework for the revitalization of the free market tradition, it was Milton Friedman who articulated its most compelling appeal. Together with his wife, Rose, Friedman argued in *Capitalism and Freedom* published in 1962 that the free economic market was the *necessary* precondition of political freedom, and indeed, of human happiness and welfare generally. While capitalism can operate in an authoritarian political environment, they argued, a democratic political environment requires highly decentralized decision-making. Therefore, liberty cannot exist when decisions are made centrally as in socialism. Moreover, it is clearly threatened when the state accumulates the power to make more and more decisions which, they asserted, was occurring as the liberal state expanded its regulatory apparatus. Tying the various streams together, they concluded that the free market was the best guarantor of political freedom, economic well-being, and consumer welfare.

One can assess the impact of the free market revival by contrasting the appearance of *Capitalism and Freedom* with the Friedmans' publication of *Free to Choose* seventeen years later. While the first book enjoyed respectable sales, they were trivial compared to those of the latter book which was on the nonfiction best-seller list for many weeks. Perhaps even more importantly, Milton Friedman based a widely seen television series upon (and also entitled) *Free to Choose*. Clearly the views which revived so modestly with the publication of the first issue of the *Journal of Law and Economics* had arrived as a major force. Not only other scholarly periodicals, but important corporate financed think tanks such as the Hoover Institution, the American Enterprise Institute, and the Center for the Study of American Business now churn out large quantities of well done, influential studies denouncing government regulation in virtually every area it has reached. The business press and mass media regularly attack government "over-regulation" and expose instances of bureaucratic bungling and silly decision-making. And most important, much public opinion and political rhetoric join in the chorus.

Clearly, then, those of us who do not see the market arrangements as the answer to virtually every social and economic problem are on the defensive. And it will not do in answering the law-and-economics school to denounce its advocates as "reactionaries" or "apologists for big business." This level of discourse does not answer the arguments that have been made, nor is it accurate. For many commentators in the law-and-economics tradition denounce some forms of regulation precisely because the principal beneficiaries are business interests and the principal losers are consumers. And in some instances they are correct. Little doubt exists that the principal (but not only) beneficiaries of airline rate regulation were the large domestic carriers and that the principal beneficiaries of FCC regulation have been the television networks. The law-and-economics scholars have done much valuable work in pointing out that numerous regulations have been of no benefit to consumers or that costs often exceed benefits. Rather, the appropriate criticism of the tradition is that in their zeal to throw out the bath water, they are throwing out the baby too. Behind their many case studies lies the implication that market arrangements are superior to regulation in most, if not all, situations.

II.

The task of those opposed to what is becoming an antiregulation tidal wave is to devise a framework that will indicate when regulation may be justified and when it is not. This task is far more formidable than simply dividing regulation into social and economic categories and then lauding examples of social regulation, such as the Occupational Safety and Health Act, environmental standards, and civil rights rules while denouncing economic regulations, such as those concerning railroad rates or aviation entry controls. The simplistic dichotomy between social and economic regulation forgets the fact that all regulations involve costs as well as benefits. Simply labeling a regulation as social does not necessarily preclude a finding that its costs in some instances exceed benefits. To illustrate with an extreme hypothetical example, it is possible that government could require automobile manufacturers to develop a car that will allow a person to survive a head-on impact at one hundred miles per hour. But the costs of producing each car (or, perhaps more accurately, tank) meeting this standard might exceed $50,000, all or most of which would be passed on to consumers. The fact that every regulation carries a price tag that we will ultimately pay for as consumers and/or taxpayers indicates that simply classifying regulations into economic (bad) or social (good) categories provides a deficient framework for justifying regulation.

Rather the social-economic dichotomy is useful only *after* we are able to justify regulation as the best social arrangement to deal with a problem. For once we identify a social benefit that can generally be attained through regulation we are compelled to ask how much extra social benefit will be obtained with the application of additional costs. When the marginal benefit is less than the marginal costs, we know that the regulation has gone beyond the proper point, even though the type of regulation may be *generally* justified. In the automobile safety example, since very few of us would be willing to expend $50,000 for a new car, any standard that imposed so stringent a safety requirement would be excessive. But on the other hand, most

of us would probably be willing to spend $50 more per auto-
mobile if that expenditure greatly reduced the likelihood of a
fatality if an accident occurred while driving 55 miles per hour.
Thus, even if regulation is justified generally, it may not be
above a certain attainment level. But this argument should be
carefully kept separate from one with which it is often confused—when is regulation *generally* justified? Let us frankly
admit that some of the criticisms currently made about *particular* regulations are correct. Regulators, in their zeal, often
do not weigh marginal benefits against marginal costs; they
sometimes misallocate their resources on less important matters, and they are sometimes imperious and paternalistic. But
simply because the Occupational Safety and Health Administration (OSHA) devoted considerable effort to the trivial task
of defining ladders and setting specification standards for them,
it does not follow that government regulation of work place
safety and health is *generally* inappropriate. Indeed, too much
evidence indicates that many workers have had to suffer in-
tolerable work place conditions.

Our need, then, is for a set of criteria that will allow us to
judge when regulation is an appropriate governmental technique and when it is not. And while we should not be embarrassed by moral fervor, it should not be used as a substitute
for economic considerations. In fact as we will see, efficiency—
as a principal economic goal—is often aided through regulation. In proceeding, I will first define regulation, for the term
is often used in an ambiguous way. Following this, I will set
forth briefly the alleged virtues of the free market. The defects
of the market mechanism which will then be outlined lead to
the justifications for regulation. But an important word of caution is in order. Simply because we find a case of market failure,
it does not follow that regulation is the sole or the best alternative. Nor does it even follow that, in an imperfect world, any
form of government intervention is superior to the market, with
its imperfections, in a particular situation. Nor does space permit a detailed examination of which regulatory technique is
best in any specific situation. Rather, the purpose here is simply
to ascertain the situations in which regulation *may* be appropriate. The correct response to the generalized attack on reg-

ulation is not a generalized Pavlovian defense of regulation. It is a theory that draws distinction between appropriate and inappropriate uses of the technique.

III.

Regulation is best defined as a state-imposed limitation on the discretion that may be exercised by private sector individuals or organizations and which is supported by the threat of sanction. For example, prior to the enactment of regulations requiring safety belts in cars, manufacturers of automobiles could exercise their discretion by installing these devices, not installing them, or complying with the requests of individual purchasers. But after the law became effective, discretion was effectively taken away from vehicle manufacturers and purchasers. Manufacturers had to install safety belts, and consumers had to purchase them. Failure to do so subjected the producer to a sanction. From the definition, the first important facet of regulation follows. A regulation apportions decision-making by a specific activity between the public and private spheres. Thus in recent years automobile manufacturers have found that the discretion they may exercise over the large numbers of decisions involved in designing, producing, and marketing cars has been reduced. At the same time they are still left with considerable discretion in each of these activities.

The notion of a mixed mode of decision-making leads, then, to the question of why only some decisions can be entrusted to private hands. Asking us why the market is sometimes held to fail compels us to inquire how it is expected to operate for our benefit in the first place. Notably, even Adam Smith carved out a number of areas in which he advocated government regulation, including banking and the mandatory erection of party walls between buildings in order to retard the spread of fire. Nevertheless, most decisions are best left to the market, in his view, for reasons succinctly summarized by economist Arthur Okun:

A competitive market transmits signals to producers that reflect the values of consumers. If the manufacture and distribution of a new product is profitable, the benefits it provides to buyers necessarily exceed the costs of production. And these costs in turn measure the value of the other outputs that are sacrificed by using labor and capital to make the new product. Thus, profitability channels resources into more productive uses and pulls them away from less productive ones. The producer has the incentive to make what consumers want and make it in the least costly way.[5]

This argument assumes that the contract is the basic mechanism through which efficiency and free choice are achieved. Producers and consumers weigh alternative uses of their resources and select those they believe will maximize, respectively, wealth and welfare. Thus, producer A chooses to make phonograph records rather than piano-rolls because that corresponds to consumer preference. And he will choose process X, rather than process Y, to manufacture records because that will maximize his profit. At the same time, even if it is not anyone's conscious intention, this course of action conserves society's scarce resources. The force of competition, both with respect to other producers of the same product and with respect to producers of other goods that seek to attract consumers' dollars, provides strong incentives to satisfy consumers in terms of price, quality, service, etc. Thus, a seller of baked beans must attract consumer dollars not only from other bean sellers but also from purveyors of rice, spaghetti, and even bananas. The seller, again, has a strong incentive to satisfy his customers in price, quality, etc. since he thinks in terms of long-term profit maximization, and hence continuous repeat sales. And the same principles apply not only to sales to ultimate consumers but as well to sales to those who will use the purchases in the production processes.

While this brief summary cannot do full justice to the many arguments made by advocates of the free market, it is sufficient to raise the question of what difficulties exist in the theory that would justify state intervention through regulation in market processes. In general, there are several objections to the free market model that lead to the three principal justifications for regulation: (1) efficiency, (2) externalities, and (3) equity. Let us examine them now.

IV.

One of the fundamental premises of the free market is the existence of competition. Without actual or potential competition one of the essential underpinnings of the argument collapses. Yet there are situations in which competition cannot exist or in which sellers (and sometimes buyers) will collusively agree not to compete because they perceive that this strategy will more likely maximize their profits than will vigorous competition. The great volume of antitrust orders entered by the courts and the Federal Trade Commission against business firms for price fixing and other cartel practices attests to the fact that incentives to collude are strong. Further, business firms have sometimes succeeded in inducing government to enact statutes that legalize cartel arrangements. These include rate bureaus in the transportation industries and mandating minimum prices for such diverse products as wine or milk. Clearly, efficiency considerations dictate support of antitrust regulation that vigorously attacks monopolizing and cartel arrangements as well as opposition to government regulation that legitimates or lessens price competition under the guise of preventing "destructive competition."

While firms themselves are sometimes responsible for eroding competition, there are also instances in which the very nature of an industry makes competition infeasible. Such industries are termed natural monopolies and include the transmission of gas, electricity, and water. Accordingly, these companies are regulated at the local level, and while specific regulatory decisions are apt to be highly complex in both rate-making and other facets of their businesses, the underlying principle is a simple one. Regulation should compel these firms to behave as if they are subject to competitive forces, even though they are not. However, very few industries are classed as natural monopolies requiring such regulation. The principal characteristics of natural monopolies include: (1) marginal costs continually decline over the range of output, (2) continuous or repeated services are delivered through more or less permanent physical connections between plants and consumers' premises (3) the service provided tends to be a necessity, (4) no close substitute products or services are available (nothing, for example, can substitute for telephone service), (5) the services are not storable so that consumers cannot utilize a stored surplus for bargaining purposes, and (6) the services are not transferable from one customer to another.

Some of the analysts in the law-and-economics tradition wish to see deregulation extend to the natural monopolies. But experience at the turn of the century tends to confirm the need for closely regulating these entities. Until shortly after the beginning of the twentieth century it was not uncommon for large cities to be served by several utilities. But, as economist Alfred Kahn reported, in virtually every case a single franchisee would emerge in each city in each of the transmission services. In addition, the competitive phase was marked by low quality service and frequent insolvencies. From this experience grew the concept that public utilities characterized by the attributes described above are natural monopolies, and since competition and its benefits could not flourish in such industries, a public agency should regulate them. In summary, then, efficiency grounds justify regulation through antitrust as well as the continued full-scale regulation of public utilities. Certainly any moves to weaken antitrust enforcement against monopolizing or cartel practices or to "deregulate" traditional public utilities should be resisted on the grounds set forth. Only when technology changes the economic characteristics of a "natural monopoly" should deregulation be considered.

While business interests and others have launched attacks on efficiency regulation, most of the recent attacks have been leveled against regulation premised on externalities and equity grounds. Let us now look at externalities. The concept of an externality can be traced back to the writings of Alfred Marshall, but the implications were worked out by the English economist A. C. Pigou in *The Economics of Welfare* (1920). The principal distinction Pigou sought to make was between situations in which an enterprise fails to receive all of the returns from its operations and those in which its costs are not entirely internalized but are borne, in part, by others who are not parties to the firm's contractual transactions. A firm, for example, might plant trees that prevent soil erosion for the entire surrounding community (a positive externality). On the other hand, a factory might spew soot on neighboring dwellings or pollute the air of the surrounding community (a negative externality). In each case costs or benefits are imposed upon persons not involved in contractual relationships with the creators of the externalities.

Externalities involve social costs—those borne by persons outside the contractual arrangement. Such costs are not borne by something abstract called society, but rather by a few or many persons or firms. Social costs can sometimes, however, be transformed into private costs—those borne by the contracting parties—through the introducton of new production techniques. For example, the installation of pollution control devices in automobiles significantly made costs private that were once largely social. From a purely economic point of view, externalities that are not included in cost calculations inexorably lead to inefficiency for reasons succinctly stated by economist Larry Ruff:

> The efficiency of competitive markets depends on the identity of private costs and social costs. As long as the. . .producer must compensate somebody for every cost imposed by his production, his profit-maximizing decisions about how much to produce, and how, will also be socially efficient decisions. . . . If wastes do affect others, then the social costs of waste disposal are not zero. Private and social costs diverge, and private profit maximizing decisions are not socially efficient.[6]

The problem of externalities, then, is one of market failure and may well be best considered in economic terms and not the moral ones so frequently used in conjunction with problems such as air and water pollution or hazardous waste disposal. Moralizing and self-righteously assessing blame obscure the principal externalities problems: how to most cheaply reduce social costs, and how to most efficiently trade off costs and benefits. For it must be remembered that most activities involving social costs also involve social benefits. The steel mill that produces smoke also produces steel, while the automobile that produces noxious emissions also provides the only reasonable mode of transportation for many Americans. Simplistically pointing the finger at polluters obscures the fact that we are also dealing with a cost-benefit problem. If, hypothetically, a *single* dwelling existed in the same vicinity as a mammoth steel mill, would it not be far cheaper to move the home rather than compel the mill to install extremely expensive equipment? Many of us, after all, will ultimately help pay for that equipment when we buy products made with steel.

It is probable that in the last fifteen years economists have devoted more attention to the externalities problem than to any other subject, save monetary policy. And with this deluge, the arguments have become increasingly complex and sophisticated. But, generally, three basic solutions for the social cost problem have been proposed: (1) taxation, (2) property rights, and (3) regulation—the technique generally favored by American public policy. Under the first of these, firms are taxed in an amount equal to the social costs they impose. But the great difficulty with this solution is that many social costs are not readily translatable into quantitative terms. Consider the great difficulty of determining with respect to a given quantity of each pollutant: (1) the cost of future medical bills, (2) tangible costs such as additional sums required for house painting, (3) property value decline, (4) damage to amenities such as parks, trees, recreational areas, and environmental appearance as well as (5) the value of psychological well-being. Consider further the fact that tastes differ widely, and economic values placed upon the more subjective factors will vary from individual to individual. When one aggregates the large number of pollution sources, each one of which embodies these and other problems, it is clear that a solution calling for a scientifically computed tax to solve the externalities problem is simply not operational.

The property rights solution is the favorite one of those who operate within the law-and-economics tradition. Government, under this property rights conception, would first determine a maximum allowable quantity for each pollutant. The next step would be to subdivide each quantity into blocks and then auction off each block as a tradable property right-to-pollute to the highest bidder, who may then contract to sell, lease, trade, etc. the right just as one may do with real estate. Since the number of rights remains constant, their value rises as industrial production increases. For the new entrant, then, there is a strong incentive to arrange its production processes so that it does not have to purchase pollution rights, while for older firms there is an incentive to sell, rather than use, the increasingly more valuable rights. In both cases, this amounts to a voluntary system in which strong incentives exist to curtail pollution. Moreover, each firm builds social cost into its own production decision without the need for intervention on the part of government agents who know little about the peculiarities of each firm or industry.

The property rights system has been criticized, too, for its inapplicability to many real-world problems. Consider automobile pollution. Can we really expect numerous pedestrians to enter into numerous contracts with numerous motorists? Transaction costs are obviously too high. And the same transaction cost problem renders the property rights solution impractical for most air and water pollution problems. Invariably, air and water pollution from various sources admix and affect whole communities. Thus, while the property rights solution may be useful when parties are relatively few, it is an unrealistic one when there are numerous parties who are apt to be involved in transactions and where the information costs in sorting out the various sources of aggregated pollution are apt to be very high. It is, therefore, a delusion to think that we can employ a property rights system to externalities in the same way that the system is used for real estate; transaction costs are often so high that trade is effectively prohibited.

Regulation, then, appears to be the least objectionable alternative to dealing with problems of social cost. It is flexible and may be combined with aspects of the other two techniques, which is precisely what the Environmental Protection Agency (EPA) is currently doing on an experimental basis. And regulation subsumes a variety of techniques that may reach particular problems. These include: (1) *prohibition*, which is appropriate when the danger and risk of an activity are so high that marginal damage exceeds marginal benefit at all levels of output; (2) *separation*, such as zoning, which can be used to plan in such a way that the contact between conflicting activities is minimized; and (3) *standards*. It may readily be conceded that standards have sometimes been unreasonable—especially those mandating specific designs and types of control equipment—and that they have sometimes led to unnecessarily costly ways of attaining goals. But there is nothing inherent in the idea of standards (especially those that only call for the achievement of certain goals rather than delineate the way in which goals are to be met) that *necessarily* leads to inefficiency or unreasonableness. It is only a question of considering the necessary trade-offs, and the EPA has been moving in this direction.

In brief, then, the free market leads to inefficiencies because of the externalities problem, and regulation is often the least objectionable way to handle the problem. Similarly, as we will now see, there are deficiencies in the basic instrument of the free market—the contract—which also lead to inefficiency that must be cured by regulation.

V.

The third broad justification for regulation, which I will call equity, is the most elusive of the three and located more within the realm of values than efficiency or externalities. Nevertheless, the equity justification can also be shown to improve economic efficiency. This justification is, however, the most pervasive of the three, covering such diverse activities as civil rights laws, regulations concerning advertising, the licensing of physicians, and mandatory testing requirements before new drugs may be marketed. What ties these and other regulatory activities together is that they all involve government intervention in the process or terms of contracts. Purchasing a product or service or entering into a labor agreement as well as the vast number of other activities under the equity justification involves contracts. For this reason it is important for us to look closely at the nature of contract and the central role it plays in the market system and its efficiency claims. After undertaking this examination, the justification for equity regulation will become clear.

The processes of negotiating and bargaining, resisting or rushing to buy—the essence of contracting—have great impact on price and the supply-demand coordinates of the market. Free contract is, therefore, supposed to be the road to allocative efficiency. It allows producers and consumers to weigh alternative uses of their resources and set those that provide maximum wealth or welfare. The contract system is supposed to increase welfare in what economists term a Paretian optimal way. Pareto optimality exists when a change occurs that makes someone better off without making others worse off. Contracts are the principal legal mechanism for achieving Pareto optimality since a free exchange, whether of a good for a good or a good for money, involves mutual satisfactions. If I part with fifty cents for an ice-cream cone, we can assume that both the store owner and I increase our satisfactions; otherwise neither of us would have voluntarily undertaken the exchange. The thing obtained is worth more to each party than the thing given. Finally, the contract system purportedly assures that each party is free to choose the way to employ his or her resources.

One cannot overstate the centrality of contract and its virtues to the law-and-economics school. Yet certain assumptions within this important concept open the door to regulation. The first of these concerns capacity to enter contracts. An underlying assumption of the contract system is that both parties are capable of understanding the substance of their agreement and rationally considering alternatives in the terms during the negotiation process. For this reason infants and mentally defective persons cannot legally make contracts; they are not deemed to know what they are doing. This does not imply that both parties are equally shrewd with respect to a particular transaction. Rather, the capacity concept is integrally related to the second major assumption of the contract system—that each side undertakes negotiations and reaches bargaining positions in an instrumentally rational manner. This entails the consideration of alternative means to the end, the relations of the end to the secondary consequences, and the relative importance of different possible ends. The process, thus, entails an attempt by each party to obtain sufficient information so as to maximize gain through the cheapest possible means. Obviously, for the foregoing system to operate in the intended manner, the courts must (and do) void contracts that are based upon fraud, force, or duress. The process of instrumentally rational thinking as well as the freedom of choice supposedly inherent in the contracting process is thwarted when one party is deliberately misled or forced to enter into a contract.

With these assumptions underlying the contract system in mind, let us now look at the equity justification for regulatory intervention in the process. The conclusion reached is that the assumptions that were just set forth are often unrealistic in the context of modern life and that a contract is often a flawed device for protecting many people. Let us begin with an example showing one of the defects in contract, and consequently in the market mechanism. Let us suppose that there is an unregulated market in the sale of drugs employed to cure or alleviate an illness. A firm devises a product that can have serious side effects in many users twenty years after ingestion, but shows no contemporaneous adverse effects. The firm, having expended considerable sums in developing the new drug, will be reluctant to reveal information that might jeopardize sales. Rather, it has a strong incentive to market the drug and hope that the long-range side effects will not be shown to be causally related to the drug. It will certainly issue *some* cautionary information, such as not to use it when drinking alcoholic beverages, and it will provide meticulous details on dosage, method of administration, etc. But it will not voluntarily reveal damaging information that it might get away with. And neither physicians nor consumers can discover the problem without expending vast sums duplicating the drug company's testing and development efforts. Realistically, one is not willing to incur $100,000 in information costs when making a $10 purchase.

The wide information disparity between buyers and sellers of increasingly complex goods and services, the enormous costs required to privately redress this gap, and the incentives that sellers sometimes have to conceal, mislead, or deceive combine to undermine the rationale of contract. A mechanism must be found to permit those who are inequitably disadvantaged by the traditional contract relationship to bargain in an instrumentally rational way. This may be done through government-mandated information requirements, standards, licensing, or some other regulatory device. But, in any event, regulation of some sort is the only way in which the inequitable disparity in information may be redressed. Again, this follows not so much because there is a disparity between the parties to a contract in resources or information—such disparities always exist—but rather because the disparity is so great *in some instances* that one of the parties is, as a practical matter, unable to make rational judgments. The same conclusion may be reached using the capacity conception. As we noted, infants and idiots are deemed incapable of making binding contracts because they lack the capacity to understand the substance of the contractual terms and are incapable of evaluating the information needed to make a reasoned judgment. But is a layman confronted with such potentially hazardous products as automobiles, drugs, etc. in any better position? The answer is a clear no. On these bases, then, regulation of information, licensing, and standards can, in many instances (but obviously not others), be justified because it actually promotes efficiency more than the free market.

The limitations of the common law contract, fraud, duress, and capacity concepts have also led to another equity justification for public intervention into the contract process. Under some circumstances the state will seek through regulation to partly redress disparities in bargaining power. Minimum wage regulation and the safety and health rulings of OSHA are premised on the substantial disparity in the bargaining power between contracting parties. But where do we draw the line? A close look at the notion of duress will help to clarify this point. If a person is forced to enter an agreement, as we noted, there is no lawful contract because a most fundamental contract principle has been violated—there was no *freely* agreed upon meeting of the minds. But duress may come about in more subtle ways than threatening to blackmail someone. It may come about because of gross inequality of bargaining power. The unskilled worker in a high unemployment area cannot bargain about the dangers posed by the machinery with which he or she will work; the alternative is starvation.

From such considerations the common law developed the concept of an unconscionable contract, the existence of which is determined by asking two questions. First, is there gross inequality of bargaining power? The wide disparity might stem from relative bargaining position and/or relative ignorance. Thus, very unskilled workers, in contrast to engineers for example, are not only in weak bargaining positions but also apt not to recognize the dangers posed by machines and materials that they must use pursuant to their contracts of employment. The second question that must be asked is whether the contract is commercially reasonable. For example, if a buyer agrees to purchase a television set for $5,000 that ordinarily sells for $500, the contract is commercially unreasonable. Not only labor contracts but contracts-of-adhesion which are printed forms carefully drafted by one party and offered on a "take-it-or-leave-it" basis, such as leases and installment sales agreements, are apt to be written in highly complex legalistic language, much of which ordinary purchasers cannot understand. Commercially unreasonable contracts are often formed in such circumstances. Again, equity considerations based upon the rationality and efficiency principles underlying contract would appear to justify public regulatory interventions.

The jump from individual difference in bargaining power to the justification for regulation based upon discrimination between groups or regions is not a very great one. The word discrimination has taken on a pejorative meaning in recent times. But technically any contract involves discrimination—making distinctions—in the precise sense of the word. Again, the problem is where to draw the line. Perhaps the best example one can use to narrow the issue is the famous one involving Jackie Robinson. Prior to his signing a Brooklyn Dodger Organization contract in 1946, there were no black baseball players in the major or minor leagues. There were no explicit organized baseball rules banning the hiring of black players, nor was there any verbal agreement among the club owners. Rather, an unwritten folkway prevailed among the club owners until the course was changed in 1946. Now the odd thing is that the overriding goal of a baseball team is to maximize wins, yet the antiblack policy was in conflict with this goal. Yet until the Dodger action, the baseball clubs did not choose the instrumentally rational way of achieving the goal of winning.

The rule drawn from this example is a simple one. From the sellers' perspective the raison d'être of the market system is to try to maximize wealth. Property and contract rules exist to serve the ultimate end. This requires instrumentally rational use of resources—land, capital, and labor. In the case of employment this boils down to the principle that individual merit should determine hiring and advancement decisions. Consequently, when the contracts into which firms enter violate the meritocratic principle by discriminating against individuals, groups, or regions, and the discrimination is in patent conflict with the organization's legitimate goals, government regulation may be called for. But the same principle does not apply to the process of consumption. Consumers, under the basic systemic rules, should be free to indulge their tastes. Thus, a producer who will not hire blacks may be subject to government regulation, but a consumer who will only purchase from white-owned stores is free to do so.

Space precludes any detailed examination of the difficulty in applying the regulatory principle of discriminatory contracts. Nor is this the place to examine critically the variety of regulatory techniques, such as affirmative action, that have been developed in this area. It is sufficient to conclude that regulations promoting the meritocratic principle are justified, and far from being an unwarranted interference in private affairs *may* actually promote efficiency. Of course, other regulations instituted under the same aegis of civil rights, such as mandatory quotas, may have the opposite effect. In this area, as in the other ones covered, the most important task is to understand the underlying justification—if any—for a type of regulation. If no reasonable justification exists, such as in the cases of airline or motor carrier entry restrictions, we should reject regulation. If a justification for regulation does exist, the next question is whether the specific regulations proposed meet the underlying rationale for the justification. Only after these preliminary inquiries can the difficult task of weighing the costs and benefits of alternative ways to confront a problem be undertaken. In part regulation is currently under successful attack because its defenders have not provided a coherent framework for determining when it is an appropriate governmental technique and when it is not. Defending the worthwhile objectives of much regulation is, unfortunately, a complex matter, but one that must be undertaken in view of the current onslaught.

NOTES

1. John Dewey, *Liberalism and Social Action* (1935; reprint, New York: Capricorn Press, 1963), p. 54.

2. Among the path-breaking articles are Gary S. Becker, "Competition and Democracy," I: pp. 105–9; R. H. Coase, "The Federal Communications Commission," II: pp. 1–40; R. H. Coase, "The Problem of Social Cost," III: pp. 1–44; George J. Stigler, "Private Vice and Public Virtue," IV: pp. 1–11; Harold Demsetz, "The Exchange and Enforcement of Property Rights," IV: pp. 11–26; Paul W. MacAvoy, "The Regulation Induced Shortage of Natural Gas," XIV (1): pp. 167–200; and Sam Peltzman, "Toward a More General Theory of Regulation," XIX (2): pp. 211–40.

3. A few of these studies are John S. McGee, "Predatory Price Cutting: The Standard Oil (N.J.) Case," I: pp. 137–69; Charles R. Plott, "Occupational Self-Regulation: A Case Study of the Oklahoma Dry Cleaners," VIII: pp. 195–222; Robert H. Bork, "Legislative Intent and the Policy of the Sherman Act," IX: pp. 7–48; Harold Demsetz, "Why Regulate Utilities?" XI: pp. 55–66.

4. Seminal examples are Gabriel Kolko *Railroads and Regulation: 1877–1916* (Princeton, N.J.: Princeton University Press, 1965); idem, *The Triumph of Conservatism* (New York: Free Press, 1963), and James Weinstein, *The Corporate Ideal in the Liberal State* (Boston: Beacon Press, 1968).

5. Arthur M. Okun, *Equality and Efficiency* (Washington, D.C.: Brookings Institution, 1975), p. 50.

6. Larry Ruff, "The Economic Common Sense of Pollution," *Public Interest* (Spring 1970), p. 72.

Michael B. Levy

VII

Liberty, Property, and Equality: Critical Reflections on the "New Property"

Liberalism, throughout its historical development, has taken many forms. Yet as long as there have been liberals, there have been *egalitarian* liberals who have demanded that liberty, property, and equality all be compatible goals.[1] In recent years, a new generation of liberals has again tried to revive this project by redefining property in an extended, egalitarian fashion. At the heart of their argument is the contention that public assistance or "welfare" is not a "gratuity" or charitable "gift" as often defined in the law, but instead a property right with all that this term implies. In essence the "new property" theorists render all men and women property owners (regardless of their private assets) and, after a fashion, place all in a condition of rough equality in the liberal polity. The "new property" concept can be traced back to two law review articles written by Charles Reich in the 1960's.[2] These articles have formed the conceptual basis for a large number of Supreme Court cases in the 1960's and 1970's,[3] and their core idea has again found favor among some political theorists.[4]

In the following essay, I shall argue that this strategy offers a false notion of property and, more importantly, undermines much of what is most worthy of support in the liberal order. However, I must emphasize that this line of argument should not be taken to represent an attack on public assistance, the welfare state, or especially the liberal egalitarian project—it is one for which I have great sympathy. Rather I am suggesting that similarly inclined theorists must first reject the "new property" analysis and strategy before they can address the problem of property and inequality in their liberal future.

LIBERAL EGALITARIANISM

When Adam delved and Eve span
Who was then the Gentleman?

This passage, so popular among the seventeenth-century mechanic and Dissenter preachers who gave birth to the utopian rhetoric of liberalism, expresses an enduring liberal belief in every human being's natural equality. Devoid of property, Eden was abundant, without class, and unmarred by the envy provoked by distinctions between mine and thine. In stark contrast, John Locke's liberal state of nature contained property, servants to do much of the work, and ultimately even money to facilitate accumulation and exchange. Locke imagined the rise of civil society well after the Fall; and subsequent liberals, like Locke's social contracters, have considered questions of property and equality in places far removed from the abundance of Eden. The very question of distributive justice, John Rawls has reminded us,[5] implies scarcity for without it the problem of just allocation disappears.

Although some might charge that the liberal egalitarian has a "natural bias"[6] against property, it is probably truer that he has a stronger antipathy to a system which would eliminate it altogether. Property, from this perspective is not unjust *qua* property, but rather in its contingent forms. This leads to calls for reform but not abolition. No doubt this ambivalence has made someone like John Rawls an enjoyable target for liberal individualists and Marxists alike. Unwilling to consider radical communitarian perspectives for fear of destroying the individual's freedom to define and pursue a life plan, yet similarly afraid of the consequences of allowing individuals to enjoy the full desert that their life plans might otherwise bring, Rawls has embodied this ambivalence completely. In this he is not unique. At least since John Stuart Mill, this tension has been apparent in all liberal egalitarian thinking, and it persists.

As the name implies, liberal theories of all varieties concentrate on creating the conditions in which individual liberty can thrive. Property as a defined sphere of private right has played an important role in liberal thinking as a barrier to state power and as a secure realm for individual human action and freedom. However, for many liberals—traditionalists like Tocqueville and libertarians like Hayek—*equality* threatens property and raises the dual spectre of undifferentiated masses and popular tyranny. Opposing this line of argument, egalitarian liberals have insisted that greater equality complemented and in fact was essential to meaningful liberty.

Individuals had an *equal* right to liberty and thus an equal right to the means necessary to develop and sustain a purposeful, autonomous life.[7]

Liberalism is committed to an end that is at once enduring and flexible; the liberation of individuals so that the realization of their capacities may be the law of their life.[8]

Liberalism is the belief that society can safely be founded on this self-directing power of personality, that it is only on this foundation that a true community can be built. . . . It rests not on the claim that A be left alone by B, but on the duty of B to treat A as a rational being.[9]

These Kantian statements of John Dewey and L. T. Hobhouse imply that the liberal political community begins conceptually with individuals (and groups of individuals) and exists for their autonomy and ends rather than for any single end of its own. However as Dewey[10] took great pains to emphasize, this position was very far from social atomism of any sort. Individuals did not form their personalities in isolation nor were they sufficient unto themselves. Personality, potential for self-fulfillment, and the capacity to choose rationally were fundamentally determined by the social structures in and with which the individual interacted. Society, in its conscious and collective activities, might choose to help develop free and productive capacities, ignore them, or constrain them. Liberal egalitarian reformers, naturally, made the case for the social use of available resources, for the sake of liberating and nurturing each individual's potential. This brought them into direct conflict with those who argued for absolute property rights and a night watchman state.

It is important to remember that these liberals, while greatly enlarging the role for collective action, remained very much apart from the communitarian or radical democratic worlds of either Marx or Rousseau. They had no desire to see individual identity subsumed under a public one, or to create a community united by a singularity of experience. Despite their emphasis on social interaction, they never idealized the individual who experienced self-transcendence within the whole or equated freedom with the internalizing of societal norms. Their freedom remained that of being capable of rational choice among a large set of available alternatives. Twentieth-century liberal egalitarians such as Hobhouse, Dewey, Hobson, Ely, and Rawls have been sensitive to the social nature of personal identity and knowledge, yet they have continued within an individualist tradition. Having been influenced by Rousseau, Hegel, and Marx, they remained the progeny of Locke and Kant.[11]

TWO VIEWS OF PROPERTY

Property, Locke emphasized, meant "life, liberty and estate," and subsequent liberals have associated property with freedom. There is a touch of irony, therefore, in Blackstone's eighteenth-century definition of property as "sole and despotic dominion which one man exercises over the external things of the world."[12] Despotic individual control over the things of the world limits the state and leaves room for greater freedom of individual action. It also limits the resources available to those who control the state, radically limiting their power in general. The effects of proprietal freedom, however, are quite unequal, leaving egalitarian liberals apprehensive about what Rawls labels the unequal "worth of liberty." Property's exclusive character increases the power of those who possess, over and against those who have nothing or very little. Their power is that much greater if the "things" possessed are the primary machines and resources of production. It takes little imagination to envision instances when those without significant property—usually more numerous and weak—must compete among themselves for access to productive resources, and are unable to negotiate terms that are adequate to sustain their own or their family's reasonable personal development. The more despotic the control, the smaller the voice of those who depend on labor may have in determining the conditions of their daily lives. Thus, the liberal egalitarian *qua* liberal needs property, but also recoils from many of its effects. This has led to a search for ways to democratize property—if at all feasible—and to create functional substitutes or equivalents.

Blackstone's definition, however, has had only a short-lived usefulness. A century before he wrote, "despotic control" would have been unconvincing as a description of the bewildering amalgam of rights in use that individuals and families could claim as their own. At least into the middle seventeenth century, primogeniture and entail, customary rights and leases, use rights in commons and fens, dower rights and other encumbrances on a proprietor's discretion all combined to make control over external "things" seem hardly despotic (no matter how unequal and harsh). To be sure Blackstone's definition reflected early capitalist values and institutions, and helped in achieving their preeminence. Yet however useful he was to his eighteenth- and nineteenth-century readers, developments in modern capitalism have again rendered his view of property an inadequate description of the real world. Stock in a limited liability corporation might entitle one to dividends, a vote in selecting management, and the right to transfer or exchange stock, but it means little in the way of controlling the uses of the machines, land, or funds which one participates in owning. Similarly, bonds, pensions, and trusts[13] are all forms of property that do not locate "despotic" control in their owners. Patents and copyrights are hardly tangible "things." The contemporary lawyer's view of property as a "bundle of rights"— borrowed from the German Historical School and popularized in the United States by legal realists such as Wesley Hohfeld and institutional economists like John R. Common[14]—provides a better fit with the facts of contemporary practice. Thus, even without considering the effect of the regulatory state on the exercise of property rights, changes in the nature of capitalism itself have eroded Blackstone's classical liberal definition of property.

For obvious reasons, liberal egalitarians have seized the bundle of rights perspective as an analytic tool useful in disaggregating the prerogatives of proprietorship, so that they may be altered and reformed.[15] John Commons, an institutionalist well versed in the historical transformations of property and contract, suggested that the right to form unions and collectively bargain was a modern property right. If we take the logic of the legal realist even further, we can abbrogate the Lockean view that property is a thing that one has wrenched from nature, and thus over which one justly exercises control. The focus shifts from property as a natural and personal right to property as a legal and conventional right existing for the common good. It is no coincidence that Adolph Berle's insightful analysis of the separation of ownership and control in joint stock corporations (with Gardiner Means in *The Modern Corporation and Private Property*, 1932) earned him an important place in the New Deal Brain Trust. Once property could be shown to be less a tangible right and more a composite set of rights, it became philosophically legitimate to distinguish the aspects of property which were socially useful from those which were not, and to suggest that only the useful remain.

The more completely the individual property owner is divorced from subjective relation to the underlying things constituting the productive mechanism of the country, the less contribution he can make to the actual process of production and the more "liquid" his wealth becomes. Superficially, perhaps, this is more desirable. While his will no longer has significance in production, it has almost complete play in consumption. If all this wealth were evenly distributed among all American families, we would be very far toward realizing the earliest simplist dreams of the forerunners of Marxian communism.

From such a situation the age old question of legitimacy fairly shrieks for solution. What is the philosophical, moral, or economic justification for this sort of property?[16]

The egalitarian implication of Adolph Berle's statement is clear. Bundle of rights theories may conform to the data of modern capitalism; they also provide a powerful weapon for an egalitarian functionalism bent on capitalism's fundamental reform.

STATUTORY ENTITLEMENTS AS PROPERTY: EGALITARIANISM'S NEW CLOTHES

Charles Reich's concept of "the new Property" gave liberal egalitarians of the last two decades a more extreme and radical version of the "bundle of rights" approach to property. Reich wrote two articles in the middle 1960's which seemed to embody perfectly the liberal egalitarian duality: respect for property as the bulwark of liberty and anguish for the unequal liberty of those who had none. Following in the legal realist tradition, Reich emphasized the conventional nature of property (a "deliberate construction of society").[17] This process was continuing as the state created new sources of income which were "steadily taking the place of traditional forms of wealth." However government "largess"—social welfare benefits, public sector jobs, licenses, access to public resources, contracts, subsidies, public services—had a status so precarious under the law that it threatened the "underpinnings of individualism and independence."[18] Whereas traditional capitalist property had helped ensure "independence, dignity and pluralism," income derived from public sector relationships remained tied to government officials who could arbitrarily terminate them. To Reich this new condition contained the seeds of a "new feudalism,"[19] and thus the end for the freedom of liberal societies.

If a reader had read the first two-thirds of Reich's original article, he might well have thought he was reading a libertarian attack on welfare state servility which was to be completed by a clarion call to return to the virtues of market and property. Yet to Reich such a resolution would have been "marching backwards," instead of "building these values into today's society."[20] Reich reasoned that these new sources of income were every bit as legitimate as those of the past—all property rights being social constructs—but they suffered from an uncertain legal status. Since government grants were usually defined as "gratuities" or "privileges" given at the pleasure of the state, recipients lacked the legal claim or "right" to due process in cases of arbitrary termination. To resolve this *constitutional* problem and ensure due process as guaranteed under the Fifth and Fourteenth Amendments, Reich argued that we needed to see public grants for what they really were—property, "new property"—which along with one's life and liberty could not be taken without full due process. This redefinition, he exclaimed, would provide a modern "economic basis for individualism," and a new egalitarian "Homestead Act for rootless twentieth century man."

A concept of right is most urgently needed with regard to benefits like unemployment compensation, public assistance and old age insurance. These benefits are based upon a recognition that misfortune and deprivation are often caused by forces beyond the control of the individual.... The aim of these benefits is to preserve the self-sufficiency of the individual, to rehabilitate him where necessary, and allow him to be a valuable member of a family and a community; in theory they represent part of the individual's rightful share in the commonwealth.[21]

A year later Reich reiterated these points concentrating on the rights of welfare recipients.

Such sources of security are no longer regarded as luxuries or gratuities; to the recipients they are essential, fully deserved and in no sense a form of charity. It is only the poor whose entitlements, although recognized by public policy, have not been effectively enforced.... Today we see poverty as the consequence of large impersonal forces.... It is closer to the truth to say that the poor are affirmative contributors to today's society, for we are so organized as virtually to compel this sacrifice by a segment of the population.[22]

Before evaluating these claims it is important to note that Reich really made two distinct points that he subsequently conflated into one. First, he claimed that the civil liberties of those whose livelihoods were tied to the public sector were endangered because they had no protection from arbitrary *ad-*

ministrative actions. Accordingly, the owner of a radio station who required a license to operate as much as a welfare mother was an easy target for coercion. Second, he declared (in part as a solution to the first point) that all forms of public "largess" were really property and ought to be redefined as such. These are two distinct arguments, however, which seem to be inextricably related only because of the language of the Fifth and Fourteenth Amendments which protect life, liberty, and property by guaranteeing due process of the law. It is necessary that these points be handled separately.

Reich's first point is compelling and consonant with the liberal concern for liberty. Done with any regularity, the political coercion of public sector dependents or clients promises severe corruption of republican government, not to mention the violation of the liberty of the individuals directly involved. The radio station that is afraid to criticize a public policy because it fears for its license ceases to be a free institution, and the welfare mother who can't support a favored political candidate for fear of retaliation ceases to be a free citizen. It is perfectly true that the criteria of eligibility for access to public resources ought to be clear; and that in instances when this is not the case, claimants ought to have recourse to the courts. One can only agree with Reich that when dependency is inevitable or inescapable, judicial strategies to guarantee due process must be available. One of the most famous "new property" cases heard by the Supreme Court, *Goldberg* v. *Kelly* (1970), provides a good example. In this case, an adminstrator canceled public assistance because he *believed* that the client had access to outside income. This was termination based on rumor. Due process, had it been available, would have established whether the administrator's suspicions were correct before assistance was terminated.

Nevertheless, to label the receipt of a grant as a *property right* in order to insure due process is a grossly disproportionate and unnecessary tactic. Our outrage in this instance stems from a sense that an individual has been treated unfairly, that procedures were and remain arbitrary, and that the potential for later abuses is great. Simply, we are concerned about the absence of due process, not the absence of a property right. To raise the injured party's claim to the status of property clouds the issue with additional normative inferences which could have been avoided by using an alternative legal strategy.[23] Moreover, the new property strategy is a weak one for extending due process because it is virtually useless in cases which do not concern property.[24]

One is led to conclude that the desire to show that public assistance is a form of property to which one is entitled rather than charity—Reich's second point—better explains his desire to label public sector relationships as property. Whether intentionally or not, Reich attempted to alter our perception of dependency rather than simply establish due process rights. To make this case he offered four arguments, each of which was flawed.

(1) **Entitlement based on "need":** "such sources of security...are no longer regarded as luxuries or gratuities; to the recipients they are essentials."[25]

While we may depend on something—including our property or our rights—for our livelihood, it is difficult to see why dependency itself establishes that something is ours. It is true that we often come to depend on something that is already ours and that we deserve to be compensated if it is taken away. Moreover, even if something is not ours, decency may well suggest that no individual or institution precipitously eliminate that which we have come to depend upon without first giving ample warning and ensuring alternatives. Nevertheless need does not establish a property right to the thing that is needed. To offer an extreme example, the fact that a heroin addict depends on X amount of heroin per day does not give him a property right to that amount. As individuals or in our collective capacities as citizens, we may feel the moral duty to offer the addict aid. Yet is is hard to label this aid "property" to which the addict is entitled. Moreover, if we should offer aid, it need not be on terms that the addict chooses, even while we have a duty to respect the potential moral autonomy of that individual. In fact, in some cases the very condition of need implies that a person is not competent to manage his own affairs, and in such cases the aid offered might be quite paternalistic.[26] Although I am not advocating such an approach in most instances, it is clear that an argument based on need could lead to consequences far different from those that Reich's libertarian rhetoric anticipated. In any case, need does not establish a property right in the thing needed and as a basis for a claim may invite paternalistic intervention.

(2) Entitlement based on "desert": "... to the recipients they are essentials fully deserved."[27]

It is difficult to understand Reich's argument based on desert since this was a far more positive claim than the simple contention that many who are in need are without moral blame for their predicament. To be sure many who receive public assistance have worked and paid taxes for long periods of time, and they may justly see their benefits as social insurance claims. A great deal of empirical evidence indicates that Aid for Dependent Children (AFDC) recipients have work records that closely follow swings in the business cycle. In fact, this might well provide an argument for placing much of public assistance on a social insurance footing, and for concentrating more of our energies on job creating strategies.

Yet the argument from desert is a weak justification for the assistance which is given in the many instances where there is little or no history of past contribution. A teenage mother abandoned by her husband may be said to "deserve" the support of her husband or of his family, although even this claim reveals concepts of duty foreign to the property rights language that Reich employed. Nevertheless, it is hard to understand the statement that a person in such straits has a property right to *public* assistance that is grounded in desert.

Desert is difficult to define and difficult to apply in cases of distributive justice.[28] If we deserve something because of a past contribution that we have made, then desert may not apply in many cases in which assistance is badly needed. On the other hand, if desert is based on moral attributes that all share owing to a common humanity, then it is difficult to understand what Reich meant by "fully" deserved. In fact, such usage leaves the entire category of desert quite vague and uncertain, and taken to an extreme leads us to the conclusion that everyone "deserves" an income regardless of behavior. If desert is a moral category that does not apply universally, who is to determine when it does apply? Wouldn't the very act of so discriminating obviate the claim that assistance is a property right, in that no one who uses the language of property requires the recipient of a dividend check to be morally deserving of his or her income? Moreover, if everyone has a claim on the income, and thus labor, of each of us based on our shared human traits, then it is fair to ask what claims those who pay have on the labor of those who receive? Again this leads us in directions far from the individualistic rhetoric of the first part of Reich's article and his assertion of property right.

(3) **Entitlement due as "compensation"**: "Today we see poverty as the consequence of large impersonal forces. . . we are so organized as virtually to compel this sacrifice by a segment of the population."[29]

Poverty, no one can doubt, is commonly the consequence of impersonal economic and social forces that often leave those already poor to suffer disproportionately. Restrictive monetary policy, to take a recent example, strikes those firms that are weakest first and thus hurts their already low paid work force through no fault of their own. In turn, their sacrifice may contribute to a drop in the rate of inflation which will benefit many who have suffered very little. It is fair to say that those whose unemployment is a direct consequence of a public policy which benefits everyone but spreads its burdens so unevenly are in fact victims who should receive some compensation. At a minimum, this would be an argument for extending unemployment compensation or providing lump sums to help finance retraining or a move to a region where job prospects are better. Nevertheless, to assert that all who are poor are "affirmative contributors" to our overall level of well-being by virtue of their misfortunes seems to imply the necessity of an all-inclusive "reserve army of the poor" indispensable to the proper functioning of the capitalist system. If such an analysis were to be correct, two conditions would have to be met: (1) all those in need would have to be actively seeking work and (2) they would be forced to remain unemployed for the sake of future progress. If these conditions held, the argument for compensation would resemble that of paying a fireman to sit in the fire station even when there were no fires to fight. The sadder truth is that many who receive and desperately need public assistance perform no positive function in the economic system, and may at times be a detriment to our general well-being. No doubt those in need are often innocent victims, but often they are victims of irresponsible spouses or parents whose irresponsibility may or may not be related to general social conditions.

Let me reiterate that I believe there are good moral reasons to respond to their needs, but it is hard to define their claim to a share of the collective resources as a property right, and even harder to imagine that such a redefined property right could function as a barrier against state interference in their lives.

(4) Entitlement based on the social nature of property. Property according to Reich was a "deliberate construction of society," not a "natural right."[30] In making this distinction, Reich concluded that as a legal construct, property was rather arbitrary and thus could be legitimately redistributed in any desired pattern. In emphasizing the conventional nature of property, Reich echoed many twentieth-century egalitarians. This claim was rooted in the very simple truth that property rights are legal rights which vary in their specifics from society to society. For example, all societies seem to provide for the inheritance of wealth, yet the form that the descent of property takes differs greatly according to legal and social systems. Similarly, the limited liability corporation is a legal construct, as is the right to bargain collectively. Yet Reich confused the origins of a specific type of property right with the right to specific property. It is one thing to claim that property rights take different forms in different systems of positive law, and quite another to claim that a property right in X is simply and always a result of a conscious public allocation. Individuals who hold property do so on the basis of contracts or voluntary exchanges in the market (or bequests) which have been carried out in accordance with strictly created laws and definitions. Although the state protects and enforces their claim, and defines its legal structure, it is incorrect to view the state as the sole creator and distributor of claims. Yet, Reich deduced from these social facts of property right the conclusion that government created property for everyone but the poor (who were forced to rely on insecure gratuities). This argument misconstrued a simple point and led us in an unwarranted direction.

Again, the above points should not be taken as a defense of the claims of property holders to a larger share of the benefits that they can squeeze from their assets, nor as a rejection of the affirmative duty to help those in need. They are intended only as a rejection of the claim of a property right to a specific level of well-being.

ILLIBERAL LIBERALISM

Why not just put it [the right to a guaranteed quality of life] forward as a human right? The reason seems to me quite compelling. If it is asserted as a human right separate from the property right, the whole prestige of property would work against it rather than for it.... We will get further if we treat human rights as property rights. (C. B. Macpherson, 1977)

Macpherson's Reichian logic points toward the antiliberal consequences inherent in "new property" liberalism. This is ironic in that Reich's earlier praise of property as the shield which protected the individual from the state relied on a common liberal premise that there was an analytic distinction between the state and society. Property, in the tradition to which he appealed, was guaranteed (not granted) by the state, but was part of a distinct if not autonomous societal sphere. Locke's insistence that property was prepolitical and already developed in the state of nature made this precise point, and it was fundamental to his attempt to limit sovereign power. It was the same point which made Locke so useful for the American colonists in their opposition to "taxation without representation." Locke's analysis of property as extra-political attacked the royalist contention that property was a gift from the state, i.e., a sovereign gratuity. This enabled Locke to hold property right as both an analytic and a material foundation for the anchoring of other individual rights and personal liberty. Yet the force of Macpherson and Reich is precisely the opposite. The indirect consequence of their arguments has been to return to the preliberal contention that all property is a public grant. Ironically, in attempting to convert grants into property, their argument achieves the opposite. Ultimately they have made an argument that is against property right altogether, in favor of a position that holds everything to be a public asset serving public ends.

Again, a word of caution. Rejecting the position that all assets are public does not mean that the claim of absolute property right is any more acceptable. To claim total control over all of one's assets (except for a user's fee to pay for police protection) ignores that in civil society one's wealth is partially the consequence of a huge material and human infrastructure which one did not create but which one uses and benefits from. Insofar as this infrastructure is not the product of pure voluntary exchange, individual assets are not purely and simply private even if they are not the collectivity's. Nor can one ignore the rights, often unclearly defined in the law, of those negatively affected by the exercise of property right, for example, in cases of air pollution. Nevertheless, to recognize limits on the exercise of individual rights based on externalities or other obligations and duties does not destroy the presumption in favor of a wide sphere of relative autonomy. In contrast, an analysis which views all possession as an arbitrary and contingent political artifact can sanction no autonomy whatsoever. While Reich and Macpherson may not have intended to destroy the analytic grounds of social autonomy, their arguments lead in that direction.

NEO-LOCKEAN ALTERNATIVES

The "new property" fails as a liberal egalitarian analysis because it ultimately requires a defense that undercuts the philosophical grounds of the liberal order. In effect it is a strategy that chases after equality while exploiting the language of liberty. Yet liberal egalitarians need not see liberty and equality in such antagonistic terms. In what follows, I would like to suggest an alternative, neo-Lockean approach to property that might better satisfy both sides of the liberal egalitarian dualism.

Locke hypothesized, following Scripture, that before there was property, men had held the "fruits" and the "beasts" of nature in common (2nd Treatise, V. 26). However through individual labor, men could legitimately create property.

Though the Water running in fountain be everyone's, yet who can doubt but that in the pitcher is his only who drew it out?

Yet legitimate acquisition was limited by what Robert Nozick has called "the Lockean Proviso,"[31] i.e., that all property be used rather than destroyed or left to spoil, and that acquisition leave no one worse off than if acquisition had not taken place. This last point required that land "enough and as good" and "more than the as yet unprovided could use" remain. Much like a contemporary property rights theorist, Locke believed that the gains of a proprietal system left everyone better off because of increased efficiency and productivity. Nevertheless, the right of property still required that enough unclaimed property remain that those without it might still have the option of personal acquisition. This was satisfied, he felt, because there were still "great tracts of ground to be found" in places like America.

Locke's argument may be taken many ways, as Louis Hartz's classic work on "Lockean" America has demonstrated. One plausible reading of Locke, compatible with the liberal egalitarian demand that we all have the equal right to be free and to develop our rationality, would conclude that a system of property and exchange, in its exclusivity, not prevent any individual who is physically and mentally capable of sustaining a free, rational life from having access to the means of so doing. In our contemporary context, this would require that a system of distribution provide a reasonable opportunity for all to acquire skills, find employment, and even acquire property. This requirement, as in Locke's propertied state of nature, points to the real opportunity available to each individual, and not to a final distribution of income or wealth. To be sure, guaranteeing a distribution of opportunity is still a "patterned" or "end-state" approach to distributive problems, to use Robert Nozick's phrase, and contrary to a strict and absolute right of property. Such an approach recognizes that private right remains limited by its broadest consequences.[32] Yet even Nozick's strict interpretation of right has limits. For example, he admits that the owner of the only functioning well in a desert has the duty to come to the aid of those whose wells have dried up.[33] Yet it is not beyond reason to suggest that in a modern, interdependent economy, those without access to jobs, training, or accumulated property are situated similarly to those without water in the desert. In either case, the duty is not boundless. The owner of the well is not bound to keep those whose wells have dried up once they have had a reasonable chance to find an alternative means of sustenance. Where duty ends, however, is a broad subject, too large to consider here. Nevertheless, in the huge continuum between letting persons die of thirst and maintaining them in a lifetime of dependency, there is a huge "in-between."

The emphasis on real opportunity rejects both the current libertarian call for the abolition of the positive state and the opposite "new property" claim that individuals have a property right in specific level of well-being, i.e., a mix of goods and services "which changes in accordance with the changing standards of living and the development of social consciousness in the society."[34] Opportunity, of course, requires that individuals have the means to live so that they might develop. But it is not open-ended and unconditional. This rendition of the liberal egalitarian position reiterates the right of all persons to be free and their right to the means to develop positively their potential as rational and autonomous beings. In contrast, the "new property" approach to entitlement demands a specific level of well-being regardless of one's contribution or efforts to develop capabilities that might enable one to contribute in the future. The "new property" approach paints a picture of men and women as static consumers of rights rather than as dynamic individ-

uals whose rights are connected to obligations to others, even
if only capable of being fulfilled in the future. "Opportunity"
characterized Locke's initial state of common ownership; individuals had the right to *pick* acorns and *hunt* deer. These
were rights of opportunity, rights to act, and not rights to simply receive from the labor of others. It is true that in a society
as interdependent as ours the opportunity to act may require
that we take from the labor of others. Everyone who has ever
attended a public school has done so. But this is an act of taking
which enables that same individual (at a later date) and as a
result of his personal development to give in return. Simply to
demand a certain level of well-being is to demand that some
have the right to live off the labor of others without any possibility of reciprocity. To offer opportunity, on the other hand,
is to offer a route to individual autonomy connected to a life of
work and through work, to the future well-being of others as
well.

The attack on "new property" has prevented me from discussing many of the virtues of more traditional notions of property. I would like to suggest, however, that one way to enhance
individual opportunity and positive freedom is to pay more
attention to ways in which we can expand older forms of property, although by older I do not mean simply "capitalist." For
example, Reich himself commented that individuals often see
social security as a property right. This was a suggestion that
he would have done well to have followed up. Individuals who
contribute to systems like social security or unemployment
compensation usually see their benefits as their contractual
due. Accordingly, additional social insurance programs which
might offer medical care during periods of unemployment or
funds to finance job-retraining might be worth exploring. I have
argued elsewhere that inheritance taxes, presently used as general revenue, should finance an "opportunities grant" trust fund
that would give to every individual at the time he or she reaches
the legal age of majority a sum of money to use to pay for
higher education, vocational training, an investment, or a down
payment on a first home or car.[35] This is a single, positive act
to distribute real property which would function as property
has in the past: it would allow the individual to make choices

and consider alternatives that would not have been available. Although received through the medium of the state, it would contribute to one's independence. Liberal egalitarians should also consider ways to expand employee stock ownership plans, producer's and consumer's cooperatives, and other democratic property forms that increase the distribution of property and yet allow it to remain conceptually distinct from a state gratuity.

The possibilities for creating new owners of property are far greater than I have suggested here. However, what is important from the perspective of liberal political theory is that those who profess a concern for liberty and equality stop conflating property and income into one concept. Liberals of all stripes have defended property as an irreducible means to the cherished end of individual liberty. The egalitarian liberal has reminded all liberals that property in some of its configurations also has hindered liberty. This may require that property be reformed or steps taken to distribute it better, but not that it be defined out of existence. The liberal egalitarian must remember that he seeks equal liberty, and that this requires that he take care to nurture the social fabric that promotes liberty. If this declines into the mere pursuit of equality, he may lose both.

NOTES

1. Amy Gutmann, *Liberal Equality* (Cambridge: Cambridge University Press, 1980), pp. 1-12.

2. Charles Reich, "The New Property," *Yale Law Journal* 73 (April 1964); idem, "Individual Rights and Social Welfare: The Emerging Legal Issues," *Yale Law Journal* 74 (March 1965).

3. According to Charles Donahue, "The Future of the Concept of Property Predicted from Its Past," *Nomos XXII: Property*, ed. J. Roland Pennock and John W. Chapman (New York: New York University Press, 1980), p. 59 n.6, Reich's articles were cited forty-five times in judicial decisions between 1967 and 1978. A few of the more prominent "new property" cases are *Goldberg* v. *Kelly*, 1970; *Wheeler* v. *Montgomery*, 1970; *Perry* v. *Sidermann*, 1972; *Board of Regents* v. *Roth*, 1972; *Bishop v. Wood*, 1976.

4. C. B. Macpherson, "Human Rights as Property Rights," *Dissent* 24 (Winter 1977); Raphaella Bilski, "Basic Parameters of the Welfare

146   Michael B. Levy

State," *Social Indicators Research* 3 (1976), esp. part III, "The Right to Welfare." For an attempt to explain this process rather than to legitimate it, see Kathi V. Friedman, *Legitimation of Social Rights and the Western Welfare State: A Weberian Perspective* (Chapel Hill: University of North Carolina Press, 1981).

5. John Rawls, *A Theory of Justice* (Cambridge, Mass.: Harvard University Press, 1971), p. 127, "Moderate scarcity over a broad range of situations." David Hume, *A Treatise of Human Nature*, ed. L. A. Selby-Bigge (Oxford: Oxford University Press, 1888), book III, part II, section 2.

6. Thomas L. Shaffer, "Men and Things: The Liberal Bias Against Property," *American Bar Association Journal* 57 (February 1971).

7. Gutmann, *Liberal Equality*; John Dewey, *Liberalism and Social Action* (New York: Capricorn Press, 1963), pp. 48, 32.

8. Dewey, *Liberalism and Social Action*, p. 56.

9. L. T. Hobhouse, *Liberalism* (Oxford: Oxford University Press, 1964), p. 66; for a similar, recent statement, see Bruce Ackerman, *Social Justice in the Liberal State* (New Haven: Yale University Press, 1980), pp. 163–67, 345-48.

10. Dewey, *Liberalism and Social Action*, p. 56.

11. Ibid., pp. 1-27; Gutmann, *Liberal Equality*, p. 218-29.

12. William Blackstone, *Commentaries on the Laws of England*, vol. II (Chicago: University of Chicago Press, 1979), p. 2, facsimile reprint 1766.

13. Thomas C. Grey, "The Disintegration of Property," in *Nomos XXII: Property*, ed. J. Roland Pennock and John W. Chapman, p. 74.

14. Wesley N. Hohfeld, *Fundamental Legal Conceptions* (New Haven: Yale University Press, 1923), pp. 23, 65; John R. Commons, *The Legal Foundations of Capitalism* (New York: Macmillan, 1924); Selig Perlman, "John Rodgers Commons," in Commons, *The Economics of Collective Action* (New York: Macmillan, 1951), p. 4.

15. Norman Furniss, "Property Rights and Democratic Socialism," *Political Studies* 26, no. 4 (1978), pp. 451-53.

16. Adolph A. Berle, *The American Economic Republic* (New York: Harcourt, Brace and World, 1963), pp. 29, 30.

17. Reich, "The New Property," p. 771; p. 775, "A construction designed to serve certain functions."

18. Ibid., p. 771.

19. Ibid.

20. Ibid., p. 779.

21. Ibid., p. 785.

22. Reich, "Individual Rights," p. 1255.

23. William van Alstyne, "Cracks in the New Property: Adjudicative Due Process in the Administrative State," *Cornell Law Review* 62 (1977), p. 484.

24. Ibid., pp. 484-85.

25. Reich, "Individual Rights," p. 1255; Reich, "The New Property," p. 737.

26. Norman E. Bowie, "Welfare and Freedom," *Ethics* 89, no. 3 (1979); Lester Thurow, "Government Cash Expenditures: Cash or In-Kind Aid," in *Markets and Morals*, ed. G. Dworkin, G. Bermant, and P. Brown (New York: John Wiley, 1977), pp. 96-98.

27. Reich, "Individual Rights," p. 1255.

28. Rawls, *A Theory of Justice*, pp. 73-75; James Sterba, "Justice and Desert," *Social Theory and Practice* 3, no. 1 (1974); Michael Zuckert, "Justice Deserted: A Critique of Rawls," *Polity* 13, no. 3 (Spring 1981); William Galston, *Justice and the Human Good* (Chicago: University of Chicago Press, 1980), pp. 170-90.

29. Reich, "Individual Rights," p. 1255.

30. Reich, "The New Property," p. 771.

31. Robert Nozick, *Anarchy, State and Utopia* (New York: Basic Books, 1974), pp. 178-82; Hillel Steiner, "The Natural Right to the Means of Production," *The Philosophical Quarterly* 27 (1977), pp. 45-46; Alan Goldman, "The Entitlement Theory of Distributive Justice," *The Journal of Philosophy* 73, no. 21 (1976), pp. 824-34.

32. For an attempt to ground rights in "consequences" see T. M. Scanlon, "Rights, Goals and Fairness," in Stuart Hampshire, ed., *Public and Private Morality* (Cambridge: Cambridge University Press, 1978).

33. Nozick, *Anarchy, State and Utopia*, pp. 179-80.

34. Bilski, "Basic Parameters," p. 466; cf. Alan Gewirth, *Reason and Morality* (Chicago: University of Chicago Press, 1978), pp. 246-47. "Equal rights to additive well-being...not equal rights to particular additive goods." "...the emphasis falls rather on developing for each person the means that enable him to obtain money for himself through his own agency as applied in productive work."

35. Michael B. Levy, "Liberal Egalitarianism and Inherited Wealth," *Political Theory* 11, no. 4 (1983).

James C. Dick

VIII

American Liberalism and the Use of Force

To say how liberal principles apply to foreign policy isn't easy, but liberals do seem to hold certain distinctive views about the means and ends of foreign policy. As to means, liberals have (or should have) a special abhorrence of war and violence. They know (or should know) the effects of wars on values dear to liberals, the subversion of civil liberties and encouragement of intolerance. And abroad, the liberal's special attachment to liberty militates against approval of resort to international coercion or any violation of national autonomy.

Liberals are also inclined to accept what has been called the spiral model of international relations rather than the deterrent model. That is, rather than stressing the chance that concessions will encourage an aggressor to press harder, they stress that in seeking security by imposing negative sanctions, a state may only sow suspicion and provoke hostile counteractions. While the deterrent model disregards how rarely statesmen are willing "to pay an exorbitant price for a chance at expansion" (even Hitler expected to obtain Poland without war), and how generous actions by a strong power often cement friendly relations, the spiral model can be embarrassed "when an aggressive power will not respond in kind to conciliation."[1] In less general terms, we might say that the liberal is wise in seeing the limits of the applicability of the Munich analogy, but risks naivete in too often denying its appropriateness.

As to the ends of foreign policy, in Hartzian fashion we may take American policy as being archetypally liberal, and note that since its emergence from isolationism American foreign policy has exhibited three characteristics. First, it has shown an exaggerated concern for security, a concern perhaps natural to an actor newly emerged on the world state but one that is carried to grotesque extremes when the Munich analogy is applied to Vietnam. The second characteristic is stress on the promotion of ideology and other values transcending security as a chief purpose of foreign policy—values like democracy, self-determination, and human rights. Thus Woodrow Wilson and Herbert Hoover were agreed that the world was an evil place. Hoover inferred that we should play no role in world affairs, and Wilson that we should act to make the world a better place. Finally, in adherence to perhaps the most important of liberal principles about foreign policy, Americans have explained international events by reference not to the structure of the international state system, but rather to the internal character of states, most notably their democraticness. Liberals believe that states whose actions are subject to popular control will be inclined against war.[2]

Now, what are the central issues of American foreign policy today to which these principles might be applied? Some would say they concern the provision of aid designed to reduce the inequality of nations. I take a more restricted view of American responsibilities and capabilities and propose instead that the central issue remains the use of force—when are we justified in putting at risk the lives of our citizens and those of other nations? It follows that I must consider the problems of war with the one other power that endangers American security, Russia, and the problems of intervention in smaller countries like Vietnam, Angola, Saudi Arabia, El Salvador, and Nicaragua. (Despite the recent presence of U.S. troops in Lebanon and the Sinai, I take the chief issue in the Middle East to be not the use of American armed forces but rather the use of American economic pressure on Israel to compel her to accept a comprehensive settlement under which she would vacate much of the West Bank; and America, as guarantor of the settlement, would find its responsibilities in the region to be much more onerous than they are today.) I recognize, of course, that as the case of relations with Israel suggests, interventions of great consequence may take forms other than the use of armed forces, but I think that the decision to kill and be killed has a unique significance that sets it apart from lesser decisions.

INTERVENTION

Theories of intervention (if there are any), and at any rate arguments justifying intervention, turn on the conception of security. As Kenneth Waltz observes, "The United States can justify her actions abroad in either or both of two ways. First, we can exaggerate the Russian or the communist threat and overreact to slight dangers. . . . Second, we can act for the good of other people."[3] Waltz takes for granted that all but a few "actions abroad" have no effect on American security, that American power is so great that only Soviet actions can jeopardize it, and that even they can do so only if they result in an unlikely accretion to Soviet power.

The exaggerations and eagerness to act for the good of others peaked in the early 1960's when the United States achieved the semblance of a first-strike capability against the Soviet Union and felt obliged to use its surplus of power in the interests of the people of South Vietnam. The exaggeration and eagerness were most eloquently expressed in the speeches of President Kennedy and his ally in the Senate, William Fulbright.[4] Today's liberals have, of course, learned better the lessons of Vietnam than have their liberal forerunners or their so-called conservative opponents. But their leeriness of arguments derived from pure balance-of-power considerations and their residual doubts about the adequacy of so mundane a consideration as security as a basis for policy hamper them in finding a convincing rationale for avoiding excursions into new Vietnams. They share with President Reagan the belief that the United States has a moral duty to see to it that the flame of liberty is not extinguished in Central America; they disagree with him only in seeing better that liberty is not the long suit of the military regimes north of Nicaragua. But the central strategic premise goes unchallenged, and so Walter Mondale contends that a Soviet military base in Central America would go counter to the "vital interests of our country."

Had liberals more concern with mere security and less with liberty, they might be able to discern that the cost to American security of a Soviet base can be measured in the number of planes and ships required to take out that base, that maintaining a base so far from home would cost the Soviets dearly, that the Soviets would gain less from a base in Central America than from one in the Eastern Mediterranean or South China Sea, and that the Soviets already have bases in Cuba at their disposal.[5] But so long as the premise of the so-called conservatives' case—that we have a vital interest in secure sea lanes and other paraphernalia of an earlier strategic era—goes unchallenged, liberals will be less able to disarm Reagan or avoid acquiescing in the reenactment of the Vietnam tragedy. Liberals have learned from Vietnam, but they have not shed a fear of responsibility for a small country's going red, a fear derived from a concern for the liberties of others and an expansive definition of security at odds with the realities of the bipolar nuclear balance of power.

For these reasons, it would not have been surprising if a Democratic liberal administration had been drawn eventually into the Salvadoran mire as it seems Reagan's may be. And in the Persian Gulf, an administration largely staffed by liberals who said they rejected the Munich analogy in Vietnam found themselves applying it there. They did so on the plausible assumptions that the security of Europe is a vital interest of the United States, and the security of the Gulf vital to Europe. Driven by this logic, liberals determined to create large conventional forces to be deployed in the Gulf region if at all possible, and if not to be ferried there by hugely expensive transport planes. Here the liberals' failure was one of strategic imagination, a failure to face up to the centrality of nuclear threats in deterring a reckless Soviet invasion, and to consider the implications of a blockade of vital sea lanes by a country 85 percent of whose shipping goes in and out of the Baltic and Black Seas, much of it bound for Russia's own east coast.[6]

But it is Europe itself where America's most substantial interests lie. Here America's strategy, devised by liberals in the early sixties, is "flexible response," a policy of strengthening conventional forces so as to put off resorting to nuclear weapons as long as possible. The notion is that the Russians might launch a conventional invasion of Western Europe, and that faced with a stark choice between capitulation and a catastrophic nuclear war, an American president would have to choose surrender. The only way to restore the credibilty of the American commitment to Europe is to build up conventional forces there. Furthermore, many liberals nowadays hold that before or after this buildup, the United States should renounce the first use of nuclear weapons, and let the onus of first use lie on the Soviet Union.

This policy rests on an incredible assumption, best expressed by Bernard Brodie: "The spectacle of a large Soviet field army crashing across the line into western Europe in the hope *and expectation* that nuclear weapons would not be used against it—thereby putting itself and the USSR totally at risk while leaving the choice of weapons to us—would seem to be hardly worth a second thought, let alone the complete reorganization and very considerable expansion of our own and our allies' military forces." This assumption about the course of battle rests in turn on a more basic assumption "that we can have a World War III on something like a World War II scale without thermonuclear weapons being used. This is the same as saying that existing stockpiles of nuclear weapons cannot reliably deter such a war, let alone a lesser war."[7] As Kenneth Waltz argues, an attacker expects to win and hence attacks with superior force. Thus "to mount a conventional defense against a nuclear adversary requires the assumption that an old military technolgy can prevent a new one from dominating the battlefield. This would be an historical anomaly."[8]

Now, as I shall argue in a moment, nuclear weapons have in a sense made strategy as traditionally understood obsolete. So perhaps such an anomaly is more plausible than it seems. But proponents of flexible response fail to see that rather than making a conventional attack more likely, strategic nuclear deterrents so increase the risks flowing from any attack as to make one less likely. Those who abhor war may in trying to elide new realities generate unnecessary dangers. Too many liberals in striving mightily to get away from nuclear weapons devise absurd strategies to do so. They fail to see that one cannot get away so easily and that the existence of nuclear weapons "poses certain compensatory advantages that might as well be accepted."[9] Worse, liberals' assumptions and policies can prove to be downright dangerous, for five reasons.

First, liberals insist on increasing conventional force levels. Quite aside from the sheer expense and hazards of the arms race that this course may touch off, increased conventional capabilities can be used elsewhere in the world. It may be no coincidence that the adoption of flexible response in 1961 was followed by the dispatch of troops to Vietnam in 1965. As Waltz puts the point, "capabilities seek missions." The lesson that follows is: "If you can you very well may; if you cannot, you will not; we should not be able to because we need not."[10]

Second, current NATO doctrine requires the use of nuclear weapons at the most dangerous possible time, as a desperate attempt to turn around the result of a lost conventional war, when they are least likely to bring victory and most likely to lead to uncontrolled escalation as the losing side finds its best targets beyond the battlefield. Where half-kiloton warheads directed at invading tanks early in the conflict might well lead to rapid deescalation, heavier warheads used on the verge of disaster against less militarily vital targets will more likely bring a response in kind.[11] Again, an understandable abhorrence of nuclear weapons may blind devisers of doctrine to the safest way to deal with their existence.

Third, as Germans from both major parties remarked in their response to four distinguished American liberals' proposed policy of no first use, if this new declaratory policy worked as intended, it would increase the danger of war in Europe for the simple reason that its very purpose is to remove the nuclear deterrent against a conventional invasion. As they say, the Soviet Union could again think of conventional war in Europe as possible because "it would no longer have to fear that nuclear weapons would inflict unacceptable damage to its own territory.... [No first use] would liberate the Soviet Union from the decisive nuclear risk...." Germans are surely right that no first use would, if it had any effect, raise the probability of war. In their words, "anxieties about a more probable conventional war [could replace] anxieties about the much less probable nuclear war."[12]

Fourth, the concerns of the Germans and other Europeans go further. As they perceive, no first use amounts to revising the American nuclear guarantee, limiting it "to the case of prior use of nuclear weapons by the Soviet Union" and withdrawing it "for example [when] the Federal Republic [was] in danger of being overrun conventionally." No first use "would destroy the confidence of Europeans...in the...Alliance as a community of risk, and would endanger the strategic unity of the Alliance and the security of Western Europe."[13]

This is a clear warning that should the American guarantee be revoked, to protect its security Europe would have to make nuclear provisions of its own. Why should this concern Americans? Why should they not be happy to be relieved of their burden in Europe and to have a sympathetic ally, powerful and independent, to stand beside America against Russia? In dealing with these questions the liberal makes the error of stressing the internal, cultural, and political character of states and neglecting the structure within which states act. Should the unlikely occur and a united Europe take its place in the world as a third great power, a tripolar structure would have replaced the bipolar balance that has helped prevent war between the two great powers since 1945. In such a balance, the two weaker powers are natural allies against the strongest. Cultural and economic considerations might work against the dynamics of a tripolar balance of power—though it is notoriously an unstable balance—but in any event the new balance would be markedly less stable than the old, as doubts as to who was the enemy and who was responsible for maintaining a balance of power came to the fore. It is fortunate that the forces militating against a united Europe are strong enough to negate the attempts at various times of American diplomats, most of them liberals, to foster the unity of Europe. To foster a new Europe by creating among its leaders and people a sense of betrayal would be folly. (But whether the presence of 500,000 American troops on the continent serving purposes European soldiers could fulfill as well is another question.)[14]

Fifth, the liberal doctrine of flexible response shares with the nuclear war-fighters (whose views I shall soon discuss) many of their most dubious and dangerous assumptions. It is no accident that Albert Wohlstetter, one of the most acute of the war-fighters, shares with George Ball the notion that a large conventional war could be fought in Europe under the nuclear umbrella.[15] They both therefore agree also on the need for escalation dominance, the ability to fight and prevail at any level the enemy may choose to engage in conflict. They accept this view in turn because they deny the unprecedented deterrent effect of nuclear weapons and the crucial importance of uncertainty about possible catastrophic consequences in dissuading either great power from taking risky actions, among them using conventional weapons against each other. Because of these shared views, the flexible responders and the war-fighters not only are at one in favoring larger expenditures on conventional arms but, by a similar logic, are also at one in favoring preparations for nuclear war that enable the United States to prevail at any level of escalation.

In weighing the wisdom of the use of American force in other countries, then, liberals display an unconcern for the structure of the international system and an excessive concern for the domestic politics of other countries. Their unconcern makes them oblivious to the dangers of a united Europe and of policies that feed the Europeans' sense of insecurity, and their concern inclines them to act to preserve the freedom of other peoples. Liberals abhor war, but their abhorrence sometimes blinds them as to how best to prevent it. Acceptance of an inevitable role for nuclear weapons in Europe would minimize the danger of their actual use and the likely extent of their use should disaster occur. Refusal to accept them as the decisive factor in battle today increases the risk of war and of catastrophe should war break out. And in Central America and elsewhere, a bolder acceptance of the role of force in international relations, an insistence on the supreme importance of security in the narrow sense and of the balance of power as its preservative, would open the way for liberals to make a more forthright and sturdy case against intervention than is permitted by their devotion to higher, nobler purposes of foreign policy and their failure to grasp some of the implications for intervention of the nuclear revolution and bipolarity.

NUCLEAR WAR

We have already dealt with nuclear issues in considering American intervention in Europe. But we have not considered strategic nuclear war, war involving the exchange of intercontinental missiles between the two great powers. About the conduct of such war three doctrines are widely held today—warfighting, deterrence, and disarmament. I shall argue that liberals should take the middle course, deterrence, and that they have been too ready to succumb to errors and illusions inherent in the other doctrines.

Disarmament

To represent the views to those who attack deterrence in favor of disarmament, we may take Jonathon Schell's widely acclaimed *The Fate of the Earth*,[16] the bible of many in the nuclear freeze movement and today's version of the strongly felt rejective sentiments about nuclear weapons that have for decades been widespread among American liberals. That Schell's work has been so well received is itself a sad commentary on the acumen of adherents of the movement against nuclear arms. The quality of Schell's rhetoric may be judged by this passage from his peroration: "E. M. Forster told us, 'Only connect!' Let us connect. Auden told us, 'We must love one another or die.' Let us love one another—in the present and across the divides of death and birth. Christ said...." Rereading such straining for effect, those who "have been unduly respectful" and perhaps even those who were "rapturously favorable" should not take long in coming to recognize the aptness of Theodore Draper's judgment. "The same sort of reception," he notes, "greeted that classic puerility, *The Greening of America*, also first published in *The New Yorker*. They belong to the same genre of political fantasy and millenial daydreaming. They are *Zeitgeist* books

that tell us more about their times than about anything else."[17]
Unfortunately, as I've suggested, some of Schell's ideas have
been around for some time and are likely to remain so, a persistent source of confusion and misunderstanding about how
we may best hope to survive in the nuclear era.

Strangely, one can read whole pages of Schell as making a
compelling case for the doctrine of deterrence. "To the old truth
that all men are brothers has been added the inescapable new
truth that not only on the moral but also on the physical plane
the nation that practices aggression will itself die." "There is
no need to abolish war among the nuclear powers; it is already
gone." Schell's argument is that "any war between Russia and
America would result in their mutual annihilation; therefore
the balance of deterrent power which allows the possibility of
war must be replaced by world government." The premise is
false; the prospect of annihilation might produce a cease-fire
well before missiles were launched at cities, and as I shall
explain a first strike would probably be directed largely away
from cities at second-strike forces. But Schell's premise does
contain the truth that any war greatly increases the risk of
annihilation. By turning this risk into a certainty, Schell makes
it seem even more irrational than it is in actuality. Indeed, he
makes it sound so irrational as to be virtually impossible. Schell
often reads like a deterrent theorist who has forgotten that
crises and escalation might bring the great powers to the brink
of war or past it. Stressing the certainty of destruction, he
makes it appear a decisive preventative of war.

Schell again sounds like a deterrent theorist when he lays
stress on the significance of the mere knowledge of the physical
laws that make the construction of nuclear weapons possible,
irreversibly so unless some catastrophe sets scientific knowledge back many decades. As Schell acknowledges, the warning
clock that tells the imminence of disaster will always exist, the
time that protects us being no more than that required for the
political arrangements that prevent war to fall apart. But Schell
does not acknowledge what the nuclear genie's being out of the
bottle implies about his later observation that "unless we rid
ourselves of our nuclear arsenals a holocaust not only *might*
occur but *will* occur—if not today, then tomorrow..." In all

consistency Schell must acknowledge the best we can do is forestall the inevitable doomsday, unless we can invent perfect political arrangements, perfect in the sense that they make impossible the construction of nuclear weapons for all time. Schell's own sense of underlying despair and his consequent resort to romantic posturing comes across in his remark that "in a disarmed world, we would not have eliminated the peril . . . —it is not in our power to do so—but we would at least have pitted our whole strength against it."

Schell thinks that his new political arrangements are at least an improvement on living with a deterrent balance of power. But his argument for the necessity of this improvement is a counsel of despair. A call to reexamine the foundations of political thought and reinvent politics and the world is not merely a voice crying in the wilderness. When the distance from here to there is so vast and is left uncharted, when the ultimate destination is described only in a portentous phrase or two, then we had best judge it is a voice leading us to a wilderness.

We take still less comfort in Schell's counsel when we discover it is founded on fallacies. One is his assumption that the scope of the solution to our problems—or more sensibly, the scope of the best way to cope with them—is necessarily commensurate with the extent of the catastrophe that awaits us if we fail. Extreme outcomes don't necessarily require extreme radical measures for their prevention. Schell is able to suppose they do in part because of a fallacious supposition, one Marx should have disabused us of, about how social structures come to be. Of "the system of sovereign states," Schell remarks that we, the human race, chose to live in it. But of course we did not. Had we so chosen, the implication would be we can choose to depart from it. But in fact, though we made the structure, we did not choose it, and departing from it is the more difficult. To make this departure seem more plausible, Schell conjures the concept of a deterrence system made by individuals in a state of nature who combine "their forces into a single force," thus centralizing "the means of violence while leaving the decision-making decentralized." He soon concludes that the doctrine of deterrence deploys weapons to protect national sovereignty and were this not so "they could be quickly dis-

mantled." But of course there is no combination of forces and
no centralization; there is only anarchy. And forces are not
deployed in order to protect national sovereignty; rather national sovereignty allows no means of preserving order but self-
help.

As a social psychologist, Schell is no more proficient a con-
jurer. He would preserve disarmament by relying on a "full
emotional, intellectual, spiritual, and visceral understanding
of the meaning of extinction." No wonder Schell would invent
a new politics! When has any individual's awareness of anything, let alone a whole population's, been so profound and
persistent? If few members of the freeze movement are today
so consumed by visions of the apocalypse, and this while the
menace looms large, how can the whole world find it in everyone for all time? And if it did, some portion of the world might
differ from others as to the means of preserving the peace, or
might think force needed to prevent some other disaster. Or
some believers might lose the faith. Or some might fear that
others are going to lose the faith, and act first to forestall them.
Even a more sensible social psychology is a weak reed because
the structural possibility of divided sovereignty cannot be gain-
said. Schell is reduced to saying that "the timeless appeal of
the greatest works of art, [testifying] to our common humanity"
is "one of the strongest grounds we have for supposing that a
political community" embracing the whole earth is possible.
One of the strongest and embarrassingly feeble.

The fatuity of Schell's advocacy of disarmament and world
government drives him to adopt a sort of transcendental philosophy. As to whether our plight is so unique in human history
as to justify the view that the new era transcends the old, Schell
wavers a little. On the one hand, "extinction is unique. . . because
it destroys mankind as the source of all possible human subjects." But on the other hand, *radical* evil—like Hitler's or
Stalin's—"goes beyond destroying individual victims (in whatever numbers) and, in addition, mutilates or destroys the *world*
that can in some way respond to—and thus in some measure
redeem—the deaths suffered." In the moral sense, from the
perspective of the members of the community destroyed, Schell

suggests that worlds have ended already. A sort of existential equivalent of extinction has already struck the victims of radical evil. Thus there exist precedents of a sort for extinction.

But the gravamen of Schell's case is that the prospect of extinction means that ordinary standards of judgment and ordinary politics must be transcended. "Politics, as it now exists, is even more thoroughly compromised than personal and social life by the peril of extinction." And the survival of the race has a value quite apart from the values of which it is the condition, like justice, beauty, and truth. We must take it then that the "political means of making international decisions" that Schell advocates are of a different order than any that now exist. Schell recognizes that his transcendentalism can be bent to justify the notion that "any action is permitted to prevent extinction" and repudiates it as a non sequitur. But his transcendentalism remains congenial to this notion, and dangerously so. Worse for Schell's case, his adoption of transcendentalism exposes the chasm between the actual politics the world has always known and the yet-to-be invented kind he advocates.

An errant transcendentalism also distorts Schell's appreciation of the meaning of the prospect of extinction. Again he errs both psychologically and philosophically. Schell imagines that the survivors of a holocaust who knew themselves to be the last generation on earth might well not want to go on living at all. If this were true, it would be because of the wretched conditions of life, not because of the bare knowledge that no future generations would live. On the contrary, poets and philosophers would memorialize their fate and Schells and Podhoretzes would debate the significance of a memorial that will have no future witness. And much less is it true that present generations of artists are enervated by a sense that everything they tell is a lie. Schell again distorts the way we live when he reports that the spectre of extinction "is with us in the delivery room, at the marriage ceremony, and on our deathbeds. It is the truth about the way we now live." The truth is we live no differently, the spectre does not haunt our conscious minds, and Schell adduces no evidence it works in our unconscious minds. And if it did, its likely effect might be not to induce despair but, as Schell himself remarks, to make "the fleeting things seem even more flickering, and more to be protected and cherished."

Schell errs philosophically as well, in his assertion that "all the activities of the common world—of marriage, of politics, of the arts, of learning"—would be rendered futile were extinction known to be imminent. The reasons life has meaning are independent of the prospect of extinction: because "the life of a person matters in itself: because it may matter to him and it may matter to other people . . . : [because] the relationships between persons matter in themselves and many are of value in themselves; [and because] a person may detect and accept a particular pattern in his own life [and] be guided by it."[18] Obviously the prospect of imminent extinction and still more of having no children at all truncates the patterns a person might detect. But the ordinary activities of life, far from being rendered futile and a nullity by the prospect of extinction, might matter more in themselves, not less, for being the last representatives of their type.

Schell's description of the workings of deterrence often serves better to justify a deterrent strategy or a wider range of Schell's nuclear options than mutual or unilateral disarmament. His description of his own preferred policy of universal, comprehensive disarmament contains not a word about how this scheme is to be enforced or attained. Taken by itself as a bare statement of aspiration, so far-reaching a scheme argues against itself and in favor of attainable alternatives. Schell's attempt to conjure away the realities of independent centers of national power and his reliance upon a universal religion of fear to transform the international system again might better be considered arguments in favor of alternatives than of his own scheme. Finally, Schell's description of the meaning of extinction distorts both the psychology and the meaning of life in the last generation. For practical purposes, the case against extinction is banal and obvious. It can be a philosophical interest, but Schell's version of it is vitiated by an indulgent romanticism and philosophical hypertrophy.

No doubt Schell's book has canonical status for many members of the nuclear freeze movement. Nevertheless, a freeze is only a beginning on the road to disarmament and world government, and so far as it goes the proposal makes some sense, especially when compared to the policies of the Reagan administration. A freeze improves on other arms-control proposals in its acceptance of whatever current force levels happen to be, thus avoiding disputes about what is to count as equality, an arcane exercise that serves to rationalize unneeded increases in weaponry, not only to serve as bargaining chips but also to achieve some meaningless numerical balance.

But a freeze is not an ideal arms agreement. It could over a period of decades disturb the bipolar balance of power, and might encourage Britain and France to devote increased resources to their nuclear programs. If it were discovered that some important weapons systems were defective, perhaps for reasons of age, under a freeze nothing could be done, and the nuclear balance of power might possibly tilt, probably in favor of the Soviet Union, since American weapons are older than theirs. Most important, new weapons that serve the purposes of deterrence better than a first strike could not be deployed. In particular, no new stealth bomber—a second strike weapon—could be built and small, single-warhead missiles could not replace larger, multi-warhead missiles. And the freeze would not stop advances in antisubmarine and satellite warfare. A freeze, then, while an improvement on current policies, is scarcely the best possible arms agreement. And it may be in any event that unilateral decisions about new weapons contribute more to stability or instability than do arms agreements that heighten concern about equality of numbers.

War-fighting

Schell denies the realities of the only peace possible in a nuclear world. War-fighters deny the realities of war. They can't deny that the great powers today possess weapons capable of destroying civilization in targeted countries, nor do they trouble to deny Schell's assertion that conceivable wars could make the race extinct. (They do rightly point out that since missiles began replacing bombers, the destructive power of deployed strategic forces has been significantly reduced.) Rather, war-fighters insist that the best way for the United States to prevent war is to be able to win whatever war might occur, and that nuclear wars can be won in the sense that one power will in the end be able to dictate terms to the other by brandishing its remaining superior weapons.

In the war-fighters' view, differences in nuclear power are significant even if both sides maintain secure second-strike forces. The side with superior power can reap diplomatic gains and obtain a more favorable outcome should war occur.

War-fighters believe in the necessity of escalation dominance, the capability to prevail at any level of combat. They maintain that this capability is of especial importance to the United States because of its need for "extended deterrence"— the ability to deter attacks not only on the United States but also on its allies. They envisage provocative actions like the seizure of northern Norway or of Berlin under the cover of strategic nuclear deterrence. In their most dramatic scenario, one the war-fighters return to again and again, the Russians launch a strike limited to America's land-based missiles and then dictate terms by threatening to go on to destroy cities. It would not then be rational for the United States to launch a second strike; it would be "self-deterred."

No one but a devout war-fighter finds this scenario at all plausible. The war-fighter errs in asking the question "why a country should carry out its deterrent threat. . . .[The question itself implies that the option is given serious consideration.] But in a nuclear world, a country cannot sensibly attack unless it believes that success is *assured*," because the gains it might make cannot on any plausible scenario exceed the losses it risks. Moreover, any plausible scenario must ascribe gains to one side that are of greater value to it than the other side perceives its losses to be. But is is absurd to imagine that the Russians could perceive any gain from a strike against American Minutemen that would exceed in value the cost perceived by the Americans. "Second-strike forces have to be seen in absolute terms. The question of whose interests are paramount will then determine whose will is perceived as being the stronger." Not only are aggressors unwilling to run extreme risks, but also defenders are likely to value the stakes more highly than aggressors.[19]

The argument about self-deterrence is meant to show that Soviet superiority could prevent an American retaliatory response. But the hypothesized fear is of the loss of cities, and this loss would be attributable not to superior Soviet forces but to its second-strike capability, to parity, not superiority. Better counterforce capability has meaning only in wars of attrition; in other wars the risk of losing cities is the decisive consideration.[20]

War-fighters insist that because they favor attacks on military targets they have gained the moral high ground from deterrent strategists. They say that rather than relying on threats to destroy whole cities, they favor taking full advantage of the much greater accuracy and much reduced explosive power of the newer generations of weapons to exploit to the full the obvious incentive each side has to protect its own civilian targets by not striking those of the enemy. So also they favor civil defense and antimissile weapons in space and on earth to minimize the damage war might wreak. Offensively, they favor damage limitation, that is, striking enemy weapons before they can be launched.[21]

The nuclear war that can be won would be a war of attrition, a series of exchanges aimed at military targets. In the war-fighter's view, the United States cannot adequately deter the Soviet Union unless the Soviet Union can see that it will lose a nuclear war, and the United States must therefore have sufficient strategic weapons to guarantee that at the end of a prolonged exchange it could dictate terms to the Soviet Union by threatening to use its superior remaining forces. The question "how much is enough?" in their view has no real answer; more might mean victory and less, defeat.

The war-fighting doctrine now governs the policies of the Reagan administration, as can be seen from its earlier and more candid pronouncements and from the writings of the defense intellectuals who advise it. But is is only fair to note that in earlier administrations, especially President Carter's, war-fighting objectives made substantial inroads on deterrent objectives. Presidential Directive 59, of July 1980, for instance, contemplates fighting a prolonged limited nuclear war.[22] And the Harvard Nuclear Study Group, expressing the normative liberal view in America today, endorses extended deterrence and nuclear weapons "to fight a nuclear war,...limit damage..., control escalation, provide support for American foreign policy, reassure American allies, [and] prevent Soviet nuclear coercion."[23] I have myself argued in favor of smaller nuclear weapons to control escalation. But the Harvard Group and other liberals go far toward legitimating a nuclear arsenal of indefinite size. They underestimate and misconceive, I think, the effectiveness of a purely deterrent force. It is with the case against war-fighting and for a deterrent force and doctrine that I conclude.

Deterrence

Deterrence is not to be confused with defense. "Deterrence is achieved not through the ability to defend but through the ability to punish. Purely deterrent forces provide no defense....Purely defensive forces provide no deterrence. They offer no means of punishment [except the 'punishment' of defeat in battle, which might possibly result in negligible losses]."[24] A hydrogen bomb directed at an enemy city does little to defend the country from which it is launched, but punishes the other country greatly. Nuclear missiles come close to being pure deterrent weapons. This characteristic was recognized early in the nuclear age by Bernard Brodie: "Thus far, the chief purpose of our military establishment has been to win wars. From now on its chief purpose must be to avert them. It can have almost no other useful purpose."[25] The doctrine of deterrence, then, is a radical one in that it supplants strategy in the traditional sense and replaces it with devices to avert war and to minimize the damage it wreaks if it occurs. The war-fighter's error is to uphold a tradition in new conditions where it makes no sense.

The war-fighter's conception of nuclear war cannot withstand scrutiny. It is only near the end of a counterforce war of attrition that a country can take its society out of hostage and gain the benefits of its destruction of the opponent's forces. In the meanwhile, it will have suffered as much as the opponent. And the counterforce scenario presupposes that each side will be able and willing to exercise immense restraint and control in the use of its forces, and will do so throughout a time of unprecedented torment.[26]

How does the deterrent theorist's view of the nature of war differ from the war-fighter's? Since "deterrence rests on what countries *can* do to each other with strategic nuclear weapons..., one easily leaps [as do Jonathan Schell and George Ball] to the...conclusion...that deterrent strategies [carried through] will produce a catastrophe." But should deterrence fail, deterrent strategists hold, "leaders will have the strongest incentives to keep force under control and limit damage." Military targets would be struck before industry, and industry before population. Not in the war-fighter's futile attempt to significantly "reduce the Soviet Union's ability to hurt us," but to punish it in a way that threatens still more punishment. The war-fighter has no place to stop short of victory; deterrent strategists stop "where one country threatens another's vital interests."[27] Were is not for their inherent futility, war-fighting strategies would increase the probability of war by heightening mutual insecurity. If a war is fought, the deterrent strategist seeks not victory but deescalation on any terms that protect narrowly defined vital interests. Rapid deescalation is the only sensible scenario should war occur for the same reason war is not likely to occur: no likely gain can outweigh certain and immediate losses and the risk of (still more) catastrophic losses.

In any kind of nuclear war, indeed of any war between the United States and the Soviet Union, the very existence of nuclear weapons would make the destruction of cities the ultimate threat. That being the case, such wars would be "competitions in risk taking." The military advantage of any strike would have less significance than the threat of escalation carried with it. Each strike would be a demonstration attack inflicting pain and punishment in itself, implicitly threatening to do more harm unless the attacker's demands are met, and increasing the chances of uncontrolled escalation. In a competition in risk-taking, what matters is not military capability so much as resolve—"each side's willingness to run high risks."[28]

If any war between nuclear powers becomes a competition in risk-taking, then escalation dominance is no guarantee of attaining one's goals. "An aggressor could attack in the face of escalation dominance if he believed that the defender would not pay...a price that includes a probability that the fighting will spread to each side's population centers. [And] a state confident of winning a military victory [on a local battlefield] could be deterred from attacking or deterred from defending against an attack by the fear that the war might spread to its homeland."[29]

But deterrent forces make pointless not only forces that would provide escalation dominance but also strategic arms races. The reason is a simple one, but no administration and few strategists, even those of a liberal bent, seem to have grasped its full implications. Suppose that each of two states possesses a capability to inflict unacceptable damage—say, in the case of the United States, to strike the ten largest cities in Russia and thereby destroy a quarter of its industrial capacity and kill a quarter of its population. Less damage would be done only if the attacking power chose to restrain itself. Suppose further that this capability cannot be reduced by any plausible action of the other power, and that the security of this capability is not affected by even substantial increases in the relative power of one or the other state. Then any provocative action by either state risks losses which are by definition unacceptable. Two conclusions follow. Since even the smallest risk of catastrophic losses can be outweighed only by the most certain and sizable of gains, each state will behave with great caution. And, second, this cautious behavior makes sense regardless of the relative balance of power, as long as the absolute ability to inflict unacceptable losses remains intact. Hence worries about the relative balance of power are, within wide limits, misplaced. When the pertinent question is "How many cities do we expect to lose? One? Two? Ten?" then "we stop thinking about running risk and worry about how to avoid them."[30]

Disarmers underestimate the stability of the deterrent balance and can offer nothing to put in its place. War-fighters underestimate the stability of the deterrent balance and its utility in deterring risky actions other than all-out first strikes.

Unprecedented risks render actions prudent in the prenuclear age dangerous today.

I mentioned earlier Marx's belief that human beings are trapped within social structures of their own making but not choosing. Marx's way out of the trap is to destroy existing structures and for us all together to become the architects of new ones. Conservatives and anti-Marxist liberals have alike felt that in destroying existing structures we destroy ourselves—for the very Marxian reasons that what we are like is shaped by what society is like. The family, friendships, work place, neigborhood, and other apolitical, hence undemocratic, institutions furnish the sinews of selfhood; once they are destroyed the self is left isolated, vulnerable, insupportable. A liberal domestic politics will accept and foster these intermediate institutions—and their concomitant inequalities—rather than sap the sources of their strength in pursuit of a chimerical and unjust equality. A strong and defensible self can emerge only from apolitical and inegalitarian social quarters. To respect the individual liberals must not seek directly to make all individuals equal by uprooting them from given social institutions, but rather to accept the inevitability and desirability of human differences and the social institutions that preserve and foster them. The chief liberal heresy in domestic politics is to seek to equalize individuals by destroying the social sources of the differences between them.

The international analogue of intermediate institutions is the nation-state. The chief liberal heresy in international affairs is to treat the international system as if it were a domestic society wherein all individuals are citizens of the world, their membership in the state mattering less than their rights as individuals. The business of statesmen then becomes to protect those rights when their own leaders fail to do so. Balance-of-power politics is illegitimate because it serves the ends of the state, not the individual. The structure of the international system derives whatever importance it has from the status of the state as such. If states have no rights and no nonderivative status, then the structure doesn't deserve consideration. Only if intermediate institutions are seen as having an importance of their own can liberals eschew the heresy of barefoot individualism. Only if states are seen as having a nonderivative autonomy can the heresy of interventionism to rescue individual victims be eschewed. So also, only acceptance of the legitimacy of the state system can allow consideration of systemic conditions and the balance of power to be a makeweight in deliberations over policy.

In the prenuclear, multipolar world, balance-of-power politics may have required liberals to make alliances with dictatorships and wars against democracies. But under current conditions, under a nuclear bipolar balance of power, arguments centered on state security place sharp limits on intervention and on the buildup of nuclear arms. It is by embracing the legitimacy of the state and the state system that liberals can make the strongest case against intervention and for policies that minimize the chances of nuclear war.

NOTES

1. Robert Jervis, *Perception and Misperception in International Politics* (Princeton, N.J.: Princeton University Press, 1976), pp. 90, 84.

2. Kenneth N. Waltz, "America's European Policy Viewed in Global Perspective," in *The United States and Western Europe*, ed. Wolfram F. Hanrieder (Cambridge, Mass.: Winthrop, 1974), pp. 10–11, 28.

3. Kenneth N. Waltz, *Theory of International Politics* (Reading, Mass.: Addison-Wesley, 1979), pp. 199–200.

4. Ibid., pp. 200-201.

5. Richard H. Ullman, "Plain Talk on Central America," *New York Times*, 10 July 1983, p. E21.

6. Kenneth N. Waltz, "Will the Future Be Like the Past?" Annual Meeting of the American Political Science Association, August 30–31, 1980, p. 11.

7. Bernard Brodie, *War and Politics* (New York: Macmillan, 1973), pp. 404, 409.

8. Kenneth N. Waltz, "What Will the Spread of Nuclear Weapons Do to the World?" in *International Effects of the Spread of Nuclear Weapons*, ed. John Kerry King (Washington, D.C.: Government Printing Office, 1979), p. 177.

9. Brodie, *War and Politics*, p. 401.

10. Waltz, "America's European Policy," pp. 30, 31.

11. Waltz, "What Will the Spread Do?" p. 177.

12. Kurt Kaiser, George Leber, Alois Mertes, and Franz-Joseph Schulze, "Nuclear Weapons and the Preservation of Peace," *Foreign Affairs* 60 (Summer 1982), pp. 1160, 1164.

13. Ibid., p. 1162.

14. Waltz, *Theory*, pp. 202–3; "America's European Policy," pp. 24–25, 35–36.

15. George W. Ball, "The Cosmic Bluff," *New York Review of Books*, 21 July 1983, pp. 37–41; Albert Wohlstetter, "Bishops, Statesmen, and Other Strategists on the Bombing of Innocents," *Commentary* (June 1983), p. 27.

16. Jonathan Schell, *The Fate of the Earth* (New York: Avon, 1982).

17. Theodore Draper, "How Not to Think About Nuclear War," *New York Review of Books*, 15 July 1982, p. 28.

18. Karl Britton, *Philosophy and the Meaning of Life* (Cambridge: Cambridge University Press, 1969), p. 189.

19. Kenneth N. Waltz, *The Spread of Nuclear Weapons: More May Be Better* (London: International Institute for Strategic Studies, 1982 (Adelphi Papers No. 171)), p. 18. Italics added.

20. Robert Jervis, "Why Nuclear Superiority Doesn't Matter," *Political Science Quarterly* 94 (1979–80), pp. 624–25.

21. See, e.g., Wohlstetter, "Bishops, Statesmen, and Other Strategists," pp. 15–35, and Colin S. Gray, "Nuclear Strategy: The Case for a Theory of Victory," *International Security* 4 (Summer 1979), pp. 54–87.

22. Waltz, *Spread and Nuclear Weapons*, p. 25.

23. Albert Carnesale et al., *Living With Nuclear Weapons* (New York: Bantam, 1983), pp. 156–57.

24. Waltz, "What Will the Spread Do?" p. 173.

25. Brodie, writing in 1946, cited in Schell, *Fate*, p. 197.

26. Jervis, "Why Nuclear Superiority Doesn't Matter," p. 627.

27. Waltz, *Spread of Nuclear Weapons*, p. 24.

28. Jervis, "Why Nuclear Superiority Doesn't Matter," p. 628.

29. Ibid., p. 623.

30. Waltz, "Will the Future Be Like the Past?" p. 6.

David B. Hill

IX

Rebuilding a Liberal Constituency

For political theorists, American liberalism has assumed the status of a general cultural condition. But from another perspective, liberalism is a political program. Accordingly, liberals must construct electoral platforms on which a viable and stable constituency can stand. If electoral outcomes of the late 1970's and early 1980's are any guide to the future, liberal candidates can expect some difficulty in performing this necessary task during the remainder of the decade. Nevertheless, the situation is not hopeless. Despite the much publicized defeats of several prominent liberal U.S. senators in 1978 and in 1980, and despite Ronald Reagan's self-proclaimed mandate for conservative political change in 1980, America is not running headlong to the camps of any and all conservative candidates. Yet there are discernable trends in electoral behavior which do not bode well for liberals, especially those committed to positive government actions designed to increase individual opportunity and social welfare. Any future success politicians or political parties will have in organizing and mobilizing a liberal constituency will hinge on their ability to understand the electoral problems facing liberalism and their creativity in resolving those problems.

One of the first problems that will be encountered by those

Table 1
Partisan Identification of Self-Proclaimed Liberals

	Extremely Liberal	Liberal	Slightly Liberal
Strong Democrats	30%	20%	14%
Weak Democrats	23	27	28
Independent Democrats	9	17	21
Independents	15	14	12
Independent Republicans	5	9	9
Weak Republicans	6	10	11
Strong Republicans	3	3	5
Other party	9	—	—
	100%	100%	100%

SOURCE: 1980-82 NORC General Social Surveys.

who seek to build a new liberal constituency is the decay and fragmentation of the Democratic party. For better or for worse, the immediate future of liberalism is intertwined with the Democratic party. The vitality of liberalism will quite naturally depend on the health of the principal party that houses its constituency. Problems of the Democratic party are several. First, along with the Republican party, the Democratic party is losing its members. Between the election of 1964, the apex of Democratic success in recent years, and the election of 1980, the percentage of voting age persons that identified with the Democratic party declined by 23 percent (from 51 percent in 1964 to 39 percent in 1980, according to studies by the University of Michigan's Center for Political Studies). And as Table 1 shows, liberals are among those who have deserted the party in significant numbers. Most liberals are still nominally Democrats, but a significant proportion claim to be independents or, in the case of extreme liberals, support one of the "third" parties such as the Citizen's party, John Anderson's National Unity movement, or the Libertarian party.

Another perspective on the weakened link between liberalism and the Democratic party is reflected in the fact that only 29 percent of Democratic party identifiers are liberals. Many more Democrats consider themselves moderates (42 percent) or conservatives (28 percent). Thus while we find many liberals still clinging to some semblance of Democratic partisanship, liberals may be losing influence over the future direction of their party home. In practical terms this means that liberals are losing the structure that partisanship could provide for efforts to mobilize a liberal constituency. Political parties still have a role to play in the mobilization process, but it is unrealistic to expect the Democratic party per se to become the leading element in any liberal renewal. The party has too few identifiers who will respond to simplistic partisan appeals for electoral support, and even if there were a larger Democratic majority, there would be no guarantee that it would coalesce around a liberal candidate.

Several other aspects of the nexus between liberalism and the Democratic party also pose problems. First, leaders of the party, almost all of whom are nominally liberal, seem bent on defining and redefining the brand of liberalism that will be embraced by the party, thus dividing whatever liberal consensus might exist. There are the old guard liberals, best represented by minorities and union leaders, who wish to reaffirm the party's commitment to their personal conception of the "New Deal." Challenging the control of the traditionals are bands of younger liberals, dubbed the "Atari Democrats," who are dedicated to a new vision of liberalism that emphasizes economic development and private sector solutions to economic and social problems. Standing between the traditional approaches of the New Dealers and the high-tech emphasis of the neoliberals is a fledging group of "Human Needs" liberal Democrats who combine traditional welfare state concerns with a sensitivity to the impracticality of many grandiose social welfare schemes. The presence of these disparate and competing liberal factions within the party contributes to the fragmentation of the party structure as an electoral vehicle for liberalism.

The Democratic party is weakened, too, by the declining rate of participation among some of its traditional supporters. And the trends in these declines suggest that the problem could be around for several decades to come. In particular, voting turnout has plummeted among poor and less educated whites who might have at one time voted for the Democrats. Turnout is down significantly among younger, blue-collar and service workers whom unions once might have brought into the party fold.[1] Several observers of the growing alienation among lower-status whites (as measured by Census Bureau occupational categories) suggest that this group is dissatisfied with liberal Democratic social control policies and welfare programs that are perceived to benefit blacks at the expense of working-class whites.[2] There is also evidence that class consciousness, a critical component of New Deal liberalism, is waning among lower-status whites, thus eliminating some of their motivations for political participation.[3] Whatever the cause of declining turnout among these lower-status Americans nationwide, this cannot be taken as an encouraging development for liberals and Democrats. And if it turns out that this problem festers among today's cohort of young workers, that is if younger, blue-collar workers do not develop a greater class consciousness, or they do not come to see the Democratic party as representing their interests, then liberals and Democrats stand to suffer for several decades as this large cohort of potential voters passes through the life cycle. Trends in nonparticipation can be reversed, as they were when more than 60 percent of black Chicago voters turned out to vote for Harold Washington in the 1983 Chicago mayoral election. Yet the long term trend among blue-collar workers continues unabated, a discouraging phenomenon for liberals.

In summary, the liberal constituency traditionally has been built on the foundation of a strong and vibrant political party. But owing to the weakened status of the party as we enter the last years of the century, liberalism may suffer. Certainly it would be foolhardy to suggest that liberalism cannot possibly succeed, whatever form it may take, without an affiliation with the Democratic party. Parties may well become an anachronism in the politics of the future, replaced by media and personality-oriented campaign organizations. Or one or more new political parties may emerge to house the liberal constituency. But realism begs that we do not expect such radical departures from the politics of the present. Party identification patterns change slowly, especially among the politically active, and partisanship persists as a powerful determinant of candidate choice among most voters, something John Anderson discovered in 1980.

A second problem facing liberalism is the simplicity and sometimes contradictory nature of Americans' belief systems. Furthermore, the inability or unwillingness of liberal leaders to accept the cognitive limitations of their constituencies complicates the problem. From the dawn of social psychological study of electoral behavior and public opinion, researchers have consistently found that most Americans think about politics very little and many possess practically no knowledge of some of the most rudimentary elements of public affairs.[4] According to the 1982 National Opinion Research Center (NORC) General Social Survey, only 35 percent of the population claim to keep up with public affairs "most of the time." Another 35 percent follow public affairs some of the time, while the rest never or almost never do so.

The inattentiveness of most Americans to public affairs is reflected in polls about specific knowledge of politics. Polls taken in the 1970's show, for example, that a majority of Americans could not name their congressman, did not know that the length of a congressman's term is two years (in 1978 only 30 percent knew this), did not know the two nations involved in SALT nor the meaning of "no fault" insurance, etc.[5]

More specific to ideologies is the inability of many Americans to define and use common ideological terms. In 1978 NORC asked its national sample a traditional ideological question ("Are you a liberal, moderate or conservative?"), but added the possibility for respondents to indicate that they hadn't thought very much about this or they didn't know. Nearly one in five of those polled gave one of the two latter answers indicating

that they had not developed a personal ideology along traditional lines. Similar findings emerge when respondents are
asked to define liberalism or conservatism. In the 1980 Center
for Political Studies national survey, respondents were asked
to define liberalism and conservatism. Nearly 40 percent of
those polled could not give a definition (correct or incorrect) of
either ideology. More than one in three indicated that they
hadn't thought about it, and accordingly, could not place themselves on a liberal-conservative continuum either. Other studies show that Americans do not use ideological terms (e.g.,
liberal or conservative) when they are asked to explain why
they are for or against a particular candidate. Instead, they
choose to use justifications which emphasize images, party labels, group affiliations, particular issues, or have no content
whatsoever. For example, in 1980 only 10 percent of Americans
polled by the Center for Political Studies used ideological terms
like liberalism or conservatism to explain their likes or dislikes
of Carter or Reagan.[6]

Finally, studies of the constraint, or interconnectedness, of
Americans' belief systems conclude that only a small percentage of the public possesses an ideology which is reasonably
stable over time and which is not beset by apparent internal
contradictions.[7] (I use the word apparent because the judgment
that internal contradictions exist reflects a bias toward defining
ideologies in familiar liberal or conservative terms. Alternative
methods of reconciling what appear to be inconsistencies are
rarely employed.)

Despite these well-documented limitations of the public to
think in ideological terms, many politicians attempt to build
a liberal constituency through ideological means. By this I
mean that politicians begin with an ideology that is mature
and fully developed, e.g., New Deal liberalism, and they attempt to project this full ideology into the campaign and their
political appeals. The typical New Deal liberal Democrat expects the "liberal" electorate to have internalized and accepted
all of the diverse aspects of this complex belief system, from
economic liberalism, to racial liberalism, to civil liberties, and
so forth.

Although the foregoing discussion clearly shows that this is a nearly impossible method for building a liberal constituency, or at least a winning one, politicians persist in this notion. For example, in the paragraphs above we noted that Democrats and perhaps liberals may have been hurt by declining participation of lower-status whites. In terms of certain aspects of economic liberalism this may be true. Lower-status whites might follow the New Dealers' lead in taming the power of large corporations. But these same whites might not follow the New Dealers toward racial justice and tolerance of minority viewpoints. Thus it would be possible only for a truncated New Deal appeal to mobilize lower-status whites in a single direction. Yet I imagine that there are New Dealers out there somewhere who, employing the whole body of their ideology, will try to lure these voters back to the polls and to their side during the rest of this decade. Such an appeal is bound to fail if our present understanding of the public mind is any guide to the future.

The problems of liberalism which we have outlined above suggest two guidelines for those who seek to build a new liberal constituency. First, liberalism must look beyond the boundaries of the Democratic party and enlist the support of liberal-leaning moderates and independents. Second, liberalism must acknowledge the waning salience of classical, New Deal, or other preexisting forms of liberalism, most of which are too complex for enough Americans to master. These existing forms of liberalism must be replaced by a new conceptualization of liberalism which is based on popular opinion, pragmatic in its appeals and narrow enough to support a broad, potentially winning coalition.

Undoubtedly there will be liberals who are discomforted by the second guideline inasmuch as it holds that public preferences, however simple-minded or even wrong-minded, should take some precedence over ideology in the structuring of liberal strategies. Although such a strategy will be necessary if liberals are to win elections, any greater emphasis on public opinion in the development of liberal strategies does not necessarily signal an abandonment of traditional liberal principles. As I will demonstrate in this chapter, certain elements of contemporary public opinion are perfectly compatible with earlier conceptualizations of liberalism. There are bits and pieces of the traditional liberal agendas which a majority of voters will find salient and appealing. But, unfortunately, there are also elements of traditional liberalism that the moderate to liberal public cares little about, or even opposes. Thus it seems prudent, and necessary for electoral success, that liberal candidates approach liberal constituents with the most appealing fragments of their shared ideology. Then if electoral success is achieved, there should be more than enough opportunity for liberals to work at educating the public about the desirability of the broader, more comprehensive vision of liberalism.

In the analyses which follow, it is my aim to identify the issues and publics which appear to provide the firmest foundation for building a liberal constituency in the 1980's. As I have argued above, the most prudent method of identifying issues and publics is neither through tradition nor through ideology, but rather through measurement of public opinion. Thus my own conclusions about the future of liberalism will be based on a secondary analysis of existing poll data.

Being restricted to secondary analysis of polls designed by others does pose somewhat of a restriction that should be noted. In most surveys of contemporary attitudes toward political issues and ideologies there is a distinct tendency of those constructing the surveys to be influenced by traditional conceptualizations of ideologies. Thus, instead of allowing liberals or other ideologues to establish their own agenda of issues about which to express their opinions, pollsters tend to ask questions about trendy issues that more often than not reflect preexisting visions of liberalism and conservatism: spend/save; change/preserve; more government/less government; welfare/bootstrap; and, interventionist/isolationist. This approach may be perfectly acceptable. But there is always a possibility that there are other salient issues that may be overlooked. This is especially problematic during periods when issues relevant to the public are in a state of flux, as has occurred on several occasions during the past several decades. Ecology is a good example of an issue which emerges, disappears, and then re-emerges from time to time, leaving the pollster guessing about the utility of asking those polled about their opinions concerning pollution, energy conservation, and related issues.

The survey data which I have chosen for analysis do not completely avoid the problem discussed above, but they do have several desirable characteristics that may compensate for whatever shortcomings the data may possess. The data set consists of the 1980 and 1982 General Social Survey conducted by the National Opinion Research Center. I have pooled these two surveys into a single data set, a procedure which is possible because NORC asked in both years most of the questions which I use. The resulting data set is very large—2,794 respondents— thus facilitating the analysis of smaller population sub-samples such as self-declared liberals.

Two categories of questions make the NORC studies especially useful for our purpose. First, the questions used to measure ideology and partisanship placed respondents in highly differentiated categories of each variable, e.g., "extremely liberal," "liberal," "slightly liberal," "moderate," etc. This allowed me to ascertain more precise information about the relationships between liberal identification, partisanship, and issue preferences. Second, the topics covered by the issue preference questions were not unduly narrow in their focus. Because the NORC studies are designed partially to track longitudinal change in attitudes about public issues, the General Social Surveys include questions about issues that may not necessarily still be topical in the 1980's. The only shortcoming of using the surveys (or any survey for that matter) is that they do not identify yet unknown, but emerging issues that may be critical to the formation of a liberal constituency in the latter part of the 1980's.

My strategy for identifying recruits for the new liberal constituency proceeds from two assumptions that are not unrelated. First, I believe that self-declared "liberals" must be the linchpin of any liberal revival. That is, I do not believe liberalism will rebound on the basis of some massive conversion of conservative or even moderate voters. The new coalition must have as its nucleus those persons already committed to the symbolic meanings of the label "liberal" under which the constituency will march. My emphasis on self-identified liberals does not grow out of any belief that coherent or consistent ideology is shared by those who adopt the liberal label. To the contrary, research has demonstrated quite clearly that many self-declared liberals support liberal candidates while simultaneously holding what most people might think of as rather un-liberal attitudes. Or more significantly, many liberals cannot even tell you what the label means. So it is that for many (perhaps most) Americans that ideological labels, such as "liberal," are powerful organizing elements or stimuli to political behavior, but sometimes without apparent ideological coherence.[8] Therefore, liberals must find some means of rallying their own, but perhaps without actually using prominently or extensively the liberal label in overt campaign appeals for fear of driving off the moderates necessary to constitute a winning coalition.

This leads to my second assumption, that overt campaign appeals must stress a narrow range of issues. There are several reasons for this strategy. We will see that the more issues one considers, the greater the possibility for conflict among those one seeks to unite. Persons wearing the label liberal, for example, do not agree on many issues. And because we must appeal to a broader constituency, one including moderates, in order to achieve an electoral majority, the agenda must remain narrow. By including liberals and moderates in our pool of liberal supporters, one greatly increases the possibility that focusing on too many issues might create divisions which totally undermine the prospects for a viable liberal constituency. The avoidance of conflict is not the sole reason for limiting the issues on which a liberal constituency is built, however. The widely documented inability of most voters to think in ideological terms, or even develop a strong interest in political issues, also dictates that the issues discussed be limited if the process of campaign communications is to be successful.

Given the assumptions that liberals must be the core of any new liberal constituency and that the number of issues on which this constituency will be recruited must necessarily be limited, my research strategy is relatively simple. First, we will look at the issue preferences of self-declared liberals to identify the issues on which there is a liberal consensus. Second, we will take those issues and see which ones appeal to a sufficient number of moderates and liberals to constitute a viable coalition.

Tables 2 and 3 provide us with an indication of those issues which will and will not be useful to building of a liberal constituency. In Table 2 we see that several issues which ostensibly have bound liberals together between the New Deal and the present are now dividing liberals. In particular, there seems to be division over the desirability of the welfare state and the relative preference for labor over management. On both of these issues the conventional wisdom would have projected more homogeneity among liberals (in favor of the welfare state and labor). In fact, such homogeneity can be found only among those who were "extemely liberal," but among those less avowedly liberal any consensus becomes difficult to find. Thus, the traditional view of liberal opinion may have been based on a misperception caused by the more vociferous and extreme elements of liberalism. The possibility that liberals as a whole may actually be more conservative than some have perceived is further borne out by their nearly clear-cut rejection of the legalization of marijuana and their closely divided views on abortion on demand and military buildups.

The data presented in Table 3 demonstrates that there are a few issues on which liberals hold some consensus. In general, liberals subscribe to a public interest view of government which advocates greater spending for the environment, health care, and education. There is also considerable agreement on the sanctity of civil liberties. While there may be other issues that unite self-declared liberals, issues not included in the General Social Surveys, the two issue areas identified above are the only ones that emerged in our examination of most of the major issues facing Americans in the 1980's. Although this finding may disappoint those who desire a broad consensus of liberal thought, it complements our effort to identify only a few issues on which to build a larger consensus for liberal thought.

The need to expand liberalism to other groups, most notably moderates, is requisite for any liberal resurgence. The necessity of this is made evident by the fact that in 1982 only 27 percent of the public claimed to be liberal (see Figure 1). Therefore, liberals, no matter how unified, must recruit a segment of the large portion of the public that considers itself to be moderate (41 percent in 1982). Assuming that liberalism will

Table 2
Issues that Divide Self-Proclaimed Liberals

	Percentage
Spending on Military, Armaments and Defense is . . .	
TOO LITTLE	35
ABOUT RIGHT	32
TOO MUCH	33
Spending for Welfare is . . .	
TOO LITTLE	25
ABOUT RIGHT	29
TOO MUCH	45
Spending to Improve the Condition of Blacks is . . .	
TOO LITTLE	39
ABOUT RIGHT	43
TOO MUCH	18
Abortion on Demand for any reason . . .	
APPROVE	52
DISAPPROVE	48
Government Should Reduce Income Differences . . .	
AGREE	49
DISAGREE/NEUTRAL	51
Marijuana Use Should Be Made Legal . . .	
AGREE	40
DISAGREE	60
Confidence in Leading Bankers and Financiers	78
Confidence in Leading Major Corporate Executives	82
Confidence in Union Leaders	74

SOURCE: 1980-82 NORC General Social Surveys.

Table 3
Issues that Self-Proclaimed Liberals Agree Upon

	Percentage
We are spending too little improving and protecting the environment	67
We are spending too little improving and protecting the nation's health	67
We are spending too little improving the nation's education system	64
Homosexuals should be allowed to speak in community	78
Racists should be allowed to speak in community	72
Communists should be allowed to speak in community	70
Militarists should be allowed to speak in community	69
Disapprove of wiretapping	80

SOURCE: 1980-82 NORC General Social Surveys.

continue to be housed in the Democratic party, we can safely speculate that the segment of moderates who hold the greatest prospect for liberal recruitment identify with the Democratic party or are Independents.

A strategy of directing liberal appeals to Independent and Democratic moderates and liberals seems viable, but barely so. Using the 1980–82 NORC data we find that the aforementioned block of Americans constitute merely 50.9 percent of all persons who are likely to vote in any future election. (I classified anyone who voted in 1976 or 1980 as a likely voter—a liberal assumption in several respects.) Thus if liberals can hold onto all of their own (save for liberal Republicans) and attract nearly every moderate Independent, the coalition we are discussing is viable. But any slippage among the latter group would be disastrous in that moderate Independents constitute 11.6 percent of all likely voters and more than one in five of the proposed liberal coalition.

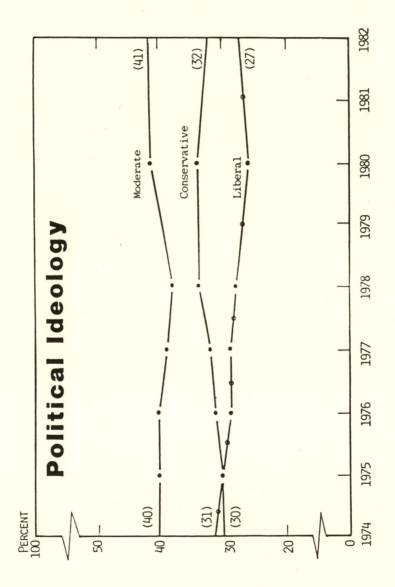

Political Ideology

PERCENT
100

50 —

40   (40)   Moderate   (41)

    (31)   Conservative   (32)
30   (30)   Liberal   (27)

20

0

1974   1975   1976   1977   1978   1979   1980   1981   1982

Assuming that any margin of liberal victory would be razor thin, which of our liberal issues (the ones liberals agree on) would best hold the coalition together? In order to answer this question I examined individual level inter-item correlations among the liberal issues. Not surprisingly, the highest inter-item correlations were between responses to the freedom of speech and civil liberties items. This suggests that one could stress freedom of speech for any group and attract virtually the same voters. The civil liberties items were much less strongly correlated with the public interest items (spending for environment, education, and health), however. And surprisingly, attitudes on the public interest spending items were only moderately correlated with each other. These findings suggest the likely fragile nature of any liberal coalition and drive home the necessity of keeping the liberal agenda both fairly narrow and palatable to moderates.

In order to assess further the likelihood that a liberal-moderate coalition stressing public interest positions and civil liberties could win elections, I constructed an index of coalition voters' agreement on these issues. The index is composed of the environment, education, and health spending items and *one* civil liberties item (allowing a Communist to speak). Each moderate and liberal Democrat and Independent was given one point on the index for each item on which he or she gave the liberal response, thus allowing index scores to range from 0 (no liberal responses) to 4 (all liberal responses). Six percent of our slim (50.9 percent) potential coalition gave no liberal responses to the four questions and 19.2 percent gave only one liberal response. Only 18.7 percent gave a liberal response to all four items. Thus, we are once again reminded that even on issues where liberals hold some consensus there is considerable breakdown in support for liberalism across the board, especially when moderates are brought into the equation. This once again underscores the massive problems associated with building a viable liberal constituency.

Using the four-item index as a guide, we can identify groups of our potential coalition that seem most resistant to the already narrow public interest oriented liberalism we have discussed. Support wanes most outside of the largest urban areas,

among middle-aged and older persons, in the South, and among
less-educated, lower-status whites. This will come as no surprise to most experienced observers of public affairs. But it is
sobering to realize that these groups are such a large chink in
the liberal's armor. Consider persons with less than a high
school education. Such persons constitute over one-fourth of
the pool of moderate and liberal Democrats and Independents
that we think liberals should recruit. But less than one-third
of the least educated pool members support three or four of our
liberal index issues. Fourteen percent support *none* of the liberal positions. Thus, it seems almost certain that many less
educated pool members will defect from liberalism and disable
efforts to build a winning liberal constituency.

What lessons have we learned from this analysis? Possibly
the most important lesson relates to the difficulty, perhaps the
impracticality, of building a new liberal constituency around
issues. Such a conclusion sounds cynical and is sure to agitate
ideologues who argue that the sure route to liberal success is
to return to "first principles" and a sense of ideological discipline. But if one places any faith in polls, then the data we
have examined must be taken as a sure sign that any return
to dogma is doomed to failure. Whatever dogma is espoused
will surely have to be fairly narrow in nature and directed
toward the sorts of public interest and civil liberties issues we
examined. And even these "most popular" issues are divisive.
More traditional and even more divisive liberal issues, such as
New Dealism, will have to be placed on the back burner of
campaign rhetoric or perhaps even discarded completely. And
liberalism must also consider the possibility that issues of any
ilk should take the back seat to candidate images and other
factors that woo voters. Indeed, in today's electoral environment, it is likely that a cohort of charismatic liberal candidates
could do more for liberalism at the ballot box than the best
issue analyses and think-tank white papers could ever accomplish. In short, images rather than issues may hold a key to
the liberal future in America.

If the future of liberalism does in fact depend more on the
recruitment of appealing office seekers than ideological refor-
mulations, the ideological core of the liberal appeal need not

be totally discarded. Rather, whenever liberals are elected to office they must recognize their responsibility to use their public trust to educate voters about the relative merits of various liberal appeals. And liberal office holders must help voters find linkages among liberal positions where none is readily apparent to the public. In short, there is much educating to do.

Consider the voter who supports the liberal position on increased spending for public education, but cannot feel any sympathy for civil libertarians' desires to allow Communists or homosexuals or racists to speak on college campuses. If liberals cannot find a method to educate a voter to the compatibility of various liberal positions such as these, then should we really be surprised that the formally uneducated and other fringe elements of the potential liberal-moderate coalition cannot reconcile the various facets of liberalism? In this respect liberals might learn from their conservative counterparts who have always been more successful in introducing conservative ideals through both formal and informal educational channels. The emphasis on "free enterprise" and "anti-communism" educational requirements that exist in many states is but one manifestation of the conservatives' successes. Another example is found in conservative "watchdog" groups that monitor the mass media for potential bias. In the matter of educational curricula, news coverage, and other wars over the minds of men and women, liberals must learn that the victories belong to the resourceful, not just the ideologically pure.

In order to succeed, liberal politicians must make special efforts to sharpen their rhetorical skills. This may be one of the greatest challenges facing liberals on account of the apparent atrophy of traditional political oratory. As one observer of contemporary political discourse has noted: "Attempts to persuade through logical reasoning have given away to attempts to manipulate audiences through psychological tactics."[9] The long, reasoned political speech of bygone eras has been supplanted by brief press statements and rehearsed press conferences which provide the press and the public with glib, superficial reassurances that "all is well." Rarely indeed is the public treated to new or challenging syntheses of political ideas whose appeals are to rational argument as opposed to base prejudice. In fairness to today's liberal (or conservative) politician, the blame for the decay in political oratory cannot be placed solely on the shortcomings of the orators. In part, this blame must be shared by the public which is, albeit by its own choice I fear, somewhat incompetent to engage in the type of political discourse which characterized the better years of political oratory.[10] Unless and until the political competence of the average citizen is elevated, it seems unlikely that even the most skilled political orators could help the public achieve new and enlightened understandings of the proper interrelationships among various tenets of liberal political thought.

It is also worth remembering that in the past, only the spectre of crisis and catastrophe has apparently caused the public to stop and listen more closely to new political ideas. One manifestation of this principle is the semiregular process of partisan realignment which takes place in America. Whenever major events such as war or severe economic calamity have plagued the nation, voters have seemed more interested in new political ideas, sometimes causing massive numbers of voters to desert the party of their forebears and the reshuffling of individual belief systems. Perhaps what liberals need today, therefore, is the same open mind to new ideas that greeted liberals' efforts in the Great Depression. In order to open voters' minds, liberal leaders must tell Americans with some urgency that the future of the nation hinges on crucial decisions made today. Perhaps then they will listen.

In this regard, one issue seems to offer liberals some hope. This issue is education and a report issued in 1982 by the National Commission on Excellence in Education provides all the ammunition necessary to mobilize the public around this issue. The report, aptly entitled, "A Nation at Risk: the Imperative for Educational Reform," makes clear that the future economic vitality, and hence the future security of the nation in an increasingly competitive international political economy, depends on our ability to improve our educational achievement. Perhaps this sort of impending crisis is what President Carter was looking for when he spoke (about the energy crisis) of "the moral equivalent of war." Most people simply yawned and ignored that appeal.[11] Why? Perhaps the president's rhetorical

skills were lacking or perhaps the public had not been suffi-
ciently informed of all the facts. But most importantly Carter
failed because the public could not make the linkages between
energy, economic development, and international security. I
imagine that a more skillful political orator could more easily
stimulate the public into thinking about education and its linkages. Moreover, education has a more personal focus for most
Americans. They can more readily see how having or not having educational opportunities can affect their own economic
successes or failures. With this personal understanding as a
foundation, liberal leaders should be able to lead the public
one step further to see the cumulative effect of educational
opportunity for millions and millions of Americans and then
for the nation as a whole. From that point it might even be
easier to draw linkages between national revival and increased
attention to public health, environmental quality, and other
elements of the public interest liberalism we discussed earlier
in this chapter. Education seems to be the desirable starting
point, however, inasmuch as the freedom and opportunity
championed by every stream of liberal thought would be served
most directly by a rededication to excellence in public education. And by making rational, reasoned appeals for economic
progress through education and other programs, liberal leaders
might once again build the constituency to which they aspire.

NOTES

The author acknowledges with gratitude the assistance of George
Edwards, Michael B. Levy, and Norman Luttbeg in the preparation
of this chapter.

    1. Howard L. Reiter, "Why Is Turnout Down?" *Public Opinion
Quarterly* (Fall 1979), pp. 297–311.
    2. Richard E. Dawson, *Public Opinion and Contemporary Disarray*
(New York: Harper & Row, 1973), p. 102; Arthur H. Miller, "Political
Issues and Trust in Government: 1964–1970," *American Political Sci-
ence Review* 68 (September 1974), pp. 951–72.
    3. The phenomenon has been demonstrated by Reiter, "Why Is
Turnout Down?" pp. 306–9.
    4. See Robert S. Erikson, Norman R. Luttbeg, and Kent L. Tedin,

American Public Opinion: Its Origins, Content and Structure (New York: John Wiley & Sons, 1980), pp. 18–33.

5. Ibid.

6. David B. Hill and Norman R. Luttbeg, *Trends in American Electoral Behavior*, 2nd ed. (Itasca, Ill.: F. E. Peacock Publishers, 1983).

7. Philip E. Converse, "The Nature of Belief Systems in Mass Publics," in *Ideology and Discontent*, ed. David Apter (New York: Free Press, 1964); George F. Bishop et al., "The Changing Structure of Mass Belief Systems: Fact or Artifact?" *The Journal of Politics* 40 (August 1978), pp. 781–87; George F. Bishop, Alfred J. Tuchfarber, and Robert W. Oldendick, "Change in the Structure of American Political Attitudes: The Nagging Question of Question Wording," *American Journal of Political Science* 22 (May 1978), pp. 250–69; and John L. Sullivan, James Piereson, and George E. Marcus, "Ideological Constraint in the Mass Public: A Methodological Critique and Some New Findings," *American Journal of Political Science* 22 (May 1978), pp. 233–49.

8. Research relevant to this point includes: Teresa E. Levitin and Warren E. Miller, "Ideological Interpretations of Presidential Elections," *American Political Science Review* 73 (September 1979), pp. 751–71; Pamela Johnson Conover and Stanley Feldman, "The Origins and Meaning of Liberal/Conservative Self-Identifications," *American Journal of Political Science* 25 (November 1981), pp. 617–45; and John D. Holm and John P. Robinson, "Ideological Identification and the American Voter," *Public Opinion Quarterly* 42 (Summer 1978), pp. 235–46.

9. Doris Graber, "Political Languages," in *Handbook of Political Communication*, ed. Dan D. Nimmo and Keith R. Sanders (Beverly Hills, Calif.: Sage Publications, 1981), p. 212.

10. Lloyd F. Bitzer, "Political Rhetoric," in *Handbook of Political Communication*, p. 247.

11. Amatai Etzioni, "The Lack of Leadership: We Found It—In Us," *National Journal* (23 February 1980), p. 336.

Selected Bibliography

Abbott, Philip. *Furious Fancies: American Political Thought in the Post Liberal Era.* Westport, Conn.: Greenwood Press, 1980.

Ackerman, Bruce. *Social Justice in the Liberal State.* New Haven: Yale University Press, 1980.

Anderson, Charles. "Political Theory and Political Science: The Rediscovery and Reinterpretation of the Pragmatic Tradition." In *What Should Political Theory Be Now?*, John Nelson, ed. Albany: SUNY Press, 1983.

Arendt, Hannah. *The Origins of Totalitarianism.* New York: Harcourt, Brace, 1951.

Bailyn, Bernard. *The Ideological Origins of the American Revolution.* Cambridge, Mass.: Harvard University Press, 1967.

Barry, Brian. *The Liberal Theory of Justice.* Oxford: Oxford University Press, 1973.

Baskin, Darryl. *American Pluralist Democracy: A Critique.* New York: D. Van Nostrand Co., 1971.

Beitzinger, A. G. *A History of American Political Thought.* New York: Harper & Row, 1972.

Bell, Daniel. *The Cultural Contradictions of Capitalism.* New York: Basic Books, Inc., 1976.

Bercovitch, Sacvan. *The Puritan Origins of the American Self.* New Haven: Yale University Press, 1975.

Berle, Adolph A., and Means, Gardiner C. *The Modern Corporation and Private Property.* New York: Macmillan, 1932.

Berlin, Isaiah. *Four Essays on Liberty*. Oxford: Oxford University Press, 1969.

Boorstin, Daniel. *The Americans: The Democratic Experience*. New York: Random House, Inc., 1974.

———. *The Genius of American Politics*. Chicago: University of Chicago Press, 1953.

Coleman, Frank. *Hobbes in America*. Toronto: University of Toronto Press, 1977.

Connolly, William, ed. *The Bias of Pluralism*. New York: Atherton, 1969.

Croly, Herbert. *The Promise of American Life*. New York: E. P. Dutton, 1963.

Curti, Merle. "The Great Mr. Locke: America's Philosopher, 1783–1861." In *The Huntington Library Bulletin* (April 1937).

Dahl, Robert. *After the Revolution: Authority in the Good Society*. New Haven: Yale University Press, 1970.

———. *A Preface to Democratic Theory*. Chicago: University of Chicago Press, 1956.

———. *Dilemmas of Pluralist Democracy*. New Haven: Yale University Press, 1982.

———. *Who Governs?* New Haven: Yale University Press, 1961.

Dewey, John. *Liberalism and Social Action*. New York: 1935, reprint, Capricorn Press, 1963.

Dick, James C. *Violence and Oppression*. Athens, Ga.: University of Georgia Press, 1979.

———. "How to Justify a Distribution of Earnings." In *Philosophy and Public Affairs* 4, no. 3 (1975).

Dworkin, Ronald. *Taking Rights Seriously*. Cambridge, Mass.: Harvard University Press, 1978.

———. "Liberalism." In *Public and Private Morality*. Stuart Hampshire, ed. New York: Cambridge University Press, 1978.

Eisenstein, Zillah. *The Radical Future of Liberal Feminism*. New York: Longman, 1981.

Ekirch, Arthur A., Jr. *The Decline of American Liberalism*. New York: Atheneum, 1969.

Elshtain, Jean Bethke. *Public Man, Private Woman: Women in Social and Political Thought*. Princeton: Princeton University Press, 1981.

Federalist Papers. Edited by Clinton Rossiter. New York: New American Library, 1961.

Fishkin, James S. *Justice, Equal Opportunity, and the Family*. New Haven: Yale University Press, 1983.

Fowler, Booth. *Believing Skeptics*. Westport, Conn.: Greenwood Press, 1978.

Fried, Charles. *Right and Wrong.* Cambridge, Mass.: Harvard University Press, 1978.

Gabriel, Ralph Henry. *The Course of American Democratic Thought.* New York: Ronald Press, 1940.

Galbraith, John Kenneth. *The New Industrial State.* New York: Signet Books, 1967.

Galston, William. "Defending Liberalism." In *American Political Science Review* 76, no. 3 (1982).

Girvetz, Harry. *The Evolution of Liberalism.* New York: Collier Books, 1963.

Goldman, Eric. *Rendezous with Destiny.* New York: Vintage, 1952.

Greenstone, J. David. *Public Values and Private Power in American Politics.* Chicago: University of Chicago Press, 1982.

Guttmann, Amy. *Liberal Equality.* Cambridge: Cambridge University Press, 1980.

Harrington, Michael. *The Twilight of Capitalism.* New York: Simon and Schuster, 1976.

Hartz, Louis. *The Liberal Tradition in America.* New York: Harcourt, Brace and World, 1955.

Hayden, Tom. "Welfare Liberalism and Social Change." In *Dissent* (1966): 75–87.

Herson, Lawrence J. R. *The Politics of Ideas: Political Theory and American Public Policy.* Homewood, Ill.: Dorsey Press, 1984.

Hill, David B., and Luttbeg, Norman R. *Trends in American Electoral Behavior,* 2nd ed. Itasca, Ill.: F. E. Peacock, 1983.

Himmelfarb, Gertrude. *On Liberty and Liberalism.* New York: Knopf, Inc., 1974.

Hobbes, Thomas. *Leviathan.* Edited by C. B. Macpherson. New York: Penguin, 1968.

Hobhouse, L. T. *Liberalism.* Oxford: Oxford University Press, 1964.

Hochschild, Jennifer. *What's Fair: American Beliefs About Distributive Justice.* Cambridge: Harvard University Press, 1981.

Hofstadter, Richard. *The American Political Tradition and the Men Who Made It.* New York: Vintage Books, 1953.

Horowitz, Robert H., ed. *The Moral Foundations of the American Republic.* Charlottesville: University Press of Virginia, 1979.

Jefferson, Thomas. *Notes on the State of Virginia.* Edited by William Peden. Chapel Hill: University of North Carolina Press, 1965.

Jouvenal, Bertrand de. *Sovereignty.* Chicago: University of Chicago Press, 1957.

Kant, Immanuel. *Foundations of the Metaphysics of Morals.* Translated by Lewis White Beck. Indianapolis: Library of Liberal Arts, 1969.

Kariel, Henry. *Beyond Liberalism: Where Relations Grow.* New York: Harper & Row, 1978.

Kaufman, Arnold. *The Radical Liberal*. New York: Simon and Schuster, Inc., 1968.

Kendall, Wilmore. *John Locke and the Doctrine of Majority Rule*. Urbana, Ill.: University of Illinois Press, 1959.

Kristol, Irving. *Two Cheers for Capitalism*. New York: Mentor Books, 1978.

Lasch, Christopher. *The Culture of Narcissism*. New York: Norton, 1978.

Lawson, Alan R. *The Failure of Independent Liberalism*. New York: Capricorn Press, 1971.

Letwin, Shirley Robin. *The Pursuit of Certainty*. Cambridge: Cambridge University Press, 1965.

Levy, Michael B. "Liberal Egalitarianism and Inherited Wealth." In *Political Theory* 11, no. 4 (1983).

———, ed. *Political Thought in America*. Homewood, Ill.: Dorsey Press, 1982.

Locke, John. *Two Treatises of Government*. Edited by Peter Laslett. New York: Mentor, 1960.

Lowi, Theodore. *The End of Liberalism*, 2nd ed. New York: Norton, 1979.

Lustig, R. Jeffrey. *Corporate Liberalism: The Origins of American Political Theory, 1890–1920*. Berkeley: University of California Press, 1982.

Macpherson, C. B. *The Life and Times of Liberal Democracy*. Oxford: Oxford University Press, 1977.

———. "Human Rights as Property Rights." In *Dissent* 24 (Winter 1977).

Mansbridge, Jane T. *Beyond Adversary Democracy*. Chicago: University of Chicago Press, 1980.

Marcuse, Herbert. *One-Dimensional Man*. Boston: Beacon Press, 1964.

Marty, Martin E. *Righteous Empire: The Protestant Experience in America*. New York: Dial, 1970.

McLoughlin, William G. *Revivals, Awakenings and Reform*. Chicago: University of Chicago Press, 1978.

McWilliams, Wilson Carey. *The Idea of Fraternity in America*. Berkeley: University of California Press, 1973.

Mill, John Stuart. *On Liberty*. Edited by Gertrude Himmelfarb. New York: Penguin, 1976.

———, and Taylor, Harriet. *Essays on Sex Equality*. Edited by Alice S. Rossi. Chicago: University of Chicago Press, 1970.

Nisbet, Robert. *The Twilight of Authority*. New York: Oxford University Press. 1975.

Nozick, Robert. *Anarchy, State and Utopia*. New York: Basic Books, 1974.

Pennock, J. Roland, and Chapman, John W., eds. *Nomos XXII: Property*. New York: New York University Press, 1980.

Pole, J. R. *The Pursuit of Equality in American History*. Berkeley: University of California Press, 1978.

Pomper, Gerald M. *Elections in America*, 2nd ed. New York: Longman, 1980.

Rawls, John. *A Theory of Justice*. Cambridge, Mass.: Harvard University Press, 1971.

———. "A Well-Ordered Society." In *Philosophy, Politics and Society*, fifth series, ed. by Peter Laslett and James Fishkin. Oxford: Basil Blackwell, 1979, pp. 6–20.

Reich, Charles. "Individual Rights and Social Welfare: The Emerging Legal Issues." In *Yale Law Journal* 74 (1965).

———. "The New Property." In *Yale Law Journal* 73 (1964).

Sandel, Michael J. *Liberalism and the Limits of Justice*. Cambridge: Cambridge University Press, 1982.

Schell, Jonathan. *The Fate of the Earth*. New York: Avon, 1982.

Stone, Alan. *Economic Regulation and the Public Interest*. Ithaca, N.Y.: Cornell University Press, 1977.

———. *Regulation and its Alternatives*. Washington, D.C.: Congressional Quarterly Press, 1982.

Tinder, Glenn. *Against Fate*. Notre Dame, Ind.: Notre Dame Press, 1981.

———. *The Crisis of Political Imagination*. New York: Scribners, 1964.

Tocqueville, Alexis de. *Democracy in America*. Translated by George Lawrence. Garden City, N.Y.: Doubleday, 1966.

Truman, David. *The Governmental Process*. New York: Knopf, 1957.

Waltz, Kenneth N. "America's European Policy Viewed in Global Perspective." In *The United States and Western Europe*. Edited by Wolfram F. Hanreider. Cambridge, Mass.: Winthrop Press, 1974.

Walzer, Michael. *Spheres of Justice*. New York: Basic Books, 1983.

Weisband, Edward. *The Ideology of American Foreign Policy: A Paradigm of Lockean Liberalism*. Beverly Hills, Calif.: Sage, 1973.

White, Morton. *Social Thought in America*. New York: Viking, 1949.

Zuckerman, Michael. *Peaceable Kingdoms: New England Towns in the Eighteenth Century*. New York: Vintage, 1970.

Index

About the Contributors

Philip Abbott is Professor of Political Science at Wayne State University. His most recent book is *The Family on Trial: Special Relationships in Modern Thought*.

Jean Bethke Elshtain is Professor of Political Science at the University of Massachusetts, Amherst. She is the author of *Public Man, Private Woman*, and editor of *The Family in Political Thought*. She has also contributed articles to *The Nation, Progressive, Commonweal*, and *Dissent* as well as to several academic journals.

James C. Dick is Associate Professor of Political Science at Wayne State University. He is the author of *Violence and Oppression*, and has published articles in *Philosophy and Public Affairs, Polity*, and the *Journal of Politics*.

Robert Booth Fowler is Professor of Political Science at the University of Wisconsin, Madison. His most recent book is *A New Engagement: Evangelical Political Thought, 1966-1976*.

David B. Hill is Associate Professor of Political Science at Texas

A&M University. He is co-author of *Trends in Electoral Analysis*.

Michael B. Levy is Associate Professor of Political Science at Texas A&M University. He is editor of *Political Thought in America: An Anthology* and has contributed articles to *Polity*, *Political Theory*, *Western Political Quarterly*, and the *Review of Politics*.

Alan Stone is Professor of Political Science at the University of Houston. He is the author of *Economic Regulation and the Public Interest* and *Regulation and Its Alternatives*.

Glenn Tinder is Professor of Political Science at the University of Massachusetts, Boston. His most recent book is *Against Fate*. He is a frequent contributor to *The New Republic*.

About the Editors

PHILIP ABBOTT is Professor of Political Science at Wayne State University. His earlier works include *Furious Fancies: American Political Thought in the Post-Liberal Era* (Greenwood Press, 1980), *The Shotgun Behind the Door: Liberalism and the Problem of Political Obligation*, and *The Family on Trial: Special Relationships in Modern Political Thought*. He has also published articles in *Political Theory*, *Review of Politics*, and *Public Administration Review*.

MICHAEL B. LEVY is Associate Professor of Political Science at Texas A&M University. He is the editor of *Political Thought in America: An Anthology* and has contributed articles to *Political Theory*, *Polity*, *Western Political Quarterly*, *Review of Politics*, and *Administration and Policy Journal*.